A Christian Lesbian Journey

Printed in the United States of America

Visit www.booksurge.com to order additional copies.

A Christian Lesbian Journey
A Continuation of Long Road to Love

Darlene Bogle

2007

A Christian Lesbian Journey

CONTENTS

This book is dedicated to my partner in love and life,
Becky Lake.

It is dedicated to the memory of my former partner
Lorrenda Des Lambson

It is also dedicated to all of the people in the Lesbian and Gay
Community who have questioned if God really loves them

Forward

I especially love the fact that this portion of the book is called *Forward*. And it's at the *beginning*. We're starting in forward motion. It's perfect for what you're about to read. Darlene Bogle's *A Christian Lesbian Journey* is forward in its honesty, it's forward in its thinking, it demonstrates moving forward in life regardless of the past, it's about bringing your heart and soul forward in your life and ultimately putting yourself forward for God to love you for who you are.

As the calendar has been moving forward, so has Darlene Bogle. Her story of self-reconciliation will blow your mind. It'll show you that it IS possible to be fully, authentically, wholly yourself in each aspect of your life. Darlene talked about when she was younger how she couldn't accept her homosexuality. This lack of self-acceptance lead her to attempt suicide, it drove her to depression and feeling numb. Fortunately her physical suicide did not succeed, but unfortunately her emotional suicide did.

Her lowered self-esteem touched every part of her life, no matter how hard she tried to hide it and seem "just fine" to friends and family members. She was deep into denial. But somehow, she did keep her spiritual self alive and began ministering to others having the same life experiences as her own. She lead an ex-gay group and became a nationally known poster girl for Exodus International. She'd talk about how she was saved by having Jesus in her life and reading the Bible consistently. What she didn't understand was that God didn't need her to minister out of denial. Minister, yes, denial of herself, no. Authenticity is important to God. Living in self-denial, is offensive to God. Reverberating denial to others…is not beneficial to anyone.

God made every one of us and as I mention in our documentary, "God don't make no junk." Actually, that phrase was on a poster I grew up with and was part of the key to my own reconciling. If God doesn't make mistakes, how could Darlene be created as a mistake? Or a choice? Or a sin? Or requiring "special rights" as a human being? Or anything negative at all? God created her. God created all of us and us telling Him he broke us and made a mistake is, well, pointless and a waste of time.

Fortunately, after 15 years of denial in Exodus, Darlene experienced her feelings and enjoyed her partner of 12 years, Des. The love story between Des and Darlene will melt any judgments away. You will see how Darlene's commitment to Des is so moving, you'll ask if you could have been as strong in the face of such adversity. The picture is still incomplete for Darlene, Des required areas of their life to continue to hide. But, here's the exciting part, as you read, you'll see this continuous theme of Darlene moving forward. Each person she met, each challenge before her, each person she continued to minister all has lead to her being the whole person she is today.

This whole book is a love story. Darlene first loved God, then she learned to love herself, then she allowed herself to love someone else. Now, she's finally reached the strongest place in her life by loving others, by honoring and being completely vulnerable, honest, authentic and OUT as a Christian lesbian. It's rare to find someone with such courage to tell this story. We're lucky as a society to have this story told. Darlene's now making up time, ministering to GLBT people across the country who are looking for a soft place to land, who knows where they are coming from as they deal with rejection and fundamentalism. Her partner Becky is so giving and such a source of strength for Darlene, she deserves credit for this book being created as well. Never take for granted unconditional love and acceptance. Darlene is a valuable asset to our yearly conferences where people get the rare opportunity to be in an intimate environment with someone who's "been there, tried that, and it doesn't work."

In a time where gay, lesbian, and transgender followers of God are spiraled into silence, Darlene Bogle steps up to the plate demonstrating that we can be ourselves. We can follow our passions. We can love and worship God. We can live in oneness. We can move *forward.*

Kim Clark and Luane Beck
Filmmakers and Educators
God & Gays: Bridging the Gap, www.godandgaysthemovie.com
God & Gays: The Conference, www.godandgaystheconference.com

What others have said about this book

I have known Darlene since the early seventies. She was just beginning to grow in her Christian walk and respond to God's call upon her life as a writer and teacher.

I believed then, as I do now, that the Holy Spirit is deeply imbedded in her heart and life journey. Helping others and sharing her heart, is one of the themes of her life. I am proud of her bravery to continue this unique journey with God. <u>A Christian Lesbian Journey</u> is just one of the ways she is helping others to grow closer to God while embracing their sexual orientation.

I am proud to call her my gay Christian sister.

Dianne Delisle M.A. Fuller Seminary

***

"A Christian Lesbian Journey" is an amazing story of commitment and desire to serve God's people that will leave a lasting impression upon your life. Once one of the leaders of the "ex-gay" movement, Darlene found that God's loving grace extended fully and without condition to the gay and lesbian (GLBT) community as well. Her "Long Road to Love" may have been further than expected, but in the end she has found the heart of God and answered the calling she was given so many years ago.

Elaine Sundby-Author Calling the Rainbow Nation Home
Webmaster of Gaychurch.org

***

Thank you Darlene for your faithfulness to the ever-widening and deepening of God's and your own heart, and for sharing so intimately with all of us. It is there, in the love and loss of relationship, in the seeking and beholding of our own truth that the divine lives. With care, courage and compassion you inspire each of us to embrace the love of God within our own selves and each another.

Dr. Tricia J. McMahon, Founder: HERS Breast Cancer Foundation, Fremont, California

***

A beautifully written story of a journey taken with intention into the truest Christian experience-love. Susan Gallagher, MFT

***

Darlene and I first met at a Christian Writer's Conference. I was a very straight, married mother of six. I was a very sheltered, devout Evangelical. Darlene, had just been 'delivered' from the gay lifestyle. All I knew about homosexuality I had either heard from the pulpit or learned from Darlene. It was wrong, it was evil, and Darlene had been healed. We read each other's manuscripts and taught at Christian conferences together. We became soul sisters and my children called her Auntie Darlene. Our friendship grew over the years.

Then one day she came to tell me that she had fallen in love. I was appalled and devastated. All I had known of homosexuality was the "Gospel According to Darlene" and according to what she had taught me she was now living in sin. During one of our many soul-searching and soul-searing discussions, Darlene, simply said, "Bon, I don't want to grow old alone .I just want to be loved." That simple heart's plea broke through all my questions and past theology.

This story is sensitive, moving, and heartbreaking all at the same time. Everyone should be so fortunate as to have a love like yours during such a horrendous experience. Your love for each other and your faith shines out bright and clear.

"Now all that I know is haze and blurred, the then I will see everything clearly, just as clearly as God sees into my heart right now. There are three things that remain-faith, hope and love-and the greatest of these is love." I Corinthians 13:12-13.

Bonnie Wheeler-Christian Author

***

This is a must-read for every person who has ever had or has breast cancer and every person who knows and loves someone who has ever had or has breast cancer.

Mary Lou Wallner, RN
Author of the Slow Miracle of Transformation

CAN'T WE FIND A WAY

To the friends I've left behind, who feel bewildered and betrayed
Who will never understand the agonizing choice I've made,
To the dear, precious loved ones, who feel they've failed somehow in me,
I sing this song of joy and grief;
I miss you, but I'm free.
Can't we find a way to make a truce of heart, if not of mind?
Can't we find a place of peace, where we can share the bread and wine?
Oh, can't we find some love to salvage? Can't we find some joy to share?
Can't we find my hand still fits in yours, to say a whispered prayer?
Oh, can't we find that just as long as God is still upon the throne,
That our hearts are hid in Jesus, and we are not our own.
To the friends I've left behind who feel bewildered and betrayed,
I love all you were to me, the memories we made.
I don't ask for your approval, Jesus footprints guide my way,
I just wish you'd let me touch you and very gently say,
Can't we find a way to make a truce of heart, if not of mind?
Can't we find a place of peace, where we can share the bread and wine?
Oh, can't we find some love to salvage? Can't we find some joy to share?
Can't we find my hand still fits in yours, to say a whispered prayer?
Oh, can't we find that just as long as God is still upon the throne,

That our hearts are hid in Jesus, and we are not our own.
Our hearts are hid in Jesus, and we are all god's own.

CHAPTER ONE
GETTING HERE FROM THERE

LOVE AT FIRST SIGHT.
The books might say there is no such thing as love at first sight; however my heart did not stop dancing since meeting Des on Saturday. I was frightened and attracted, and for the first time in many years, my thoughts were not of celibacy. I didn't know anything about her, but I couldn't stop thinking about her, and desperately wanted her to call for that counseling appointment...

Monday night, my phone rang. "Hello, this is Darlene"

There was a pause on the line. "Hello Darlene, this is Des. Do you remember who I am?"

With those words, my world was changed forever.

To be Christian and Gay seems a contradiction in the stringent theology of most mainline churches. I write the words Christian and Gay, and assume that each reader will have the same understanding. I am proud to identify myself as Christian, but not the Jerry Falwell or Pat Robertson type of Christian. I am proud to self label as a gay and Lesbian person, but cringe at the visions of the segment of my community that exploit and debase themselves at Gay Pride demonstrations across America.

I am a born again believer in Jesus Christ and have invited Him to be Lord of my life. I believe the Bible is the Word of God and make every attempt to live my life by how I interpret the principles as I understand them. Therein lays the vast chasm of difference between many Evangelicals and me.

I am a lesbian in a committed, monogamous and loving relationship with another Christian woman. I believe that God brought our lives together to bring glory to Himself that we might share His love with the Gay community and with our heterosexual brothers and sisters.

We have many gay, lesbian and trans-gendered friends who may or may not have similar spiritual beliefs. I believe they are on their own spiritual journey and will find the path of peace and acceptance without my judgment. I hope only to model the acceptance and love that I find in my relationship with Jesus Christ. This is the place I find myself as 2005 comes to an end.

My first book, Long Road to Love, A true story of hope for the Homosexual, was published in 1985. I had just turned 40, and after almost eight years of preaching, writing and speaking at national conferences, I was confident of my position on sexual orientation. I was part of a national organization called Exodus International. Their primary message was that people, who struggle with a homosexual orientation, could change. They formed support groups across the country to provide safe places for that change to occur. I knew what God thought about homosexuality, because Scripture had been interpreted and preached from their pulpits around the country. I believed the message of change being possible because of my struggle for so many years. I was no longer experiencing the conflict and attractions to women, and embraced the idea that I had changed from homosexual to heterosexual.

I had struggled with homosexual feelings since I was seventeen. I had come to believe that acting on those feelings was a sin. I immersed myself in Scripture, and found support groups to encourage my abstinence. Inside I still had nagging thoughts. *I was teaching and preaching that I was free from same sex attraction. In my heart I knew I wasn't attracted to men and any twinges of feelings toward women were shut down immediately. I had gone through deliverance and inner healing of memories. I was growing in my faith and I know that Jesus Christ is my Lord and Savior. I've committed my life, heart and ministry to Him and I know that He is fully in charge of my life. How can He bring this woman into my life? How can she be a gift from God when I'm telling others that you can't be actively gay and a Christian?* I held a full time job in the insurance industry, I was the assisting pastor at the Foursquare Church, and I directed an ex-gay ministry. I believed the message I preached. Homosexual behavior could be changed. You always had a choice whether or not to act upon feelings of same sex attraction. I was on call for counseling at any hour, both from my church and from referrals from Exodus ministries.

I believed that as I avoided the opportunity for temptation; eventually I would not be tormented with the sexual attractions for the same sex. I clung to the testimonials I heard at the Exodus conferences and saw first hand how lesbians and gay men had changed and many of them were now married.

I wasn't sure if I, or those in my group, would ever experience a change in their orientation to the point of desiring opposite sexual encounters. The primary issue as I saw it was acting out in a sexual manner.

I became the authority as it was apparent that after several years of abstinence I qualified as an "Ex-Gay". The more I spoke it, the more it was reinforced in my heart. I continued to travel, write and minister my "broken truth"

I was sincere in all that I spoke in those days. I didn't think God hated gays, or that AIDS was a judgment for a sinful lifestyle. I knew that God loved me and that He loved everyone.

In John's Gospel, 3:17 states that "God sent **not** His son into the world to condemn the world, but that the world through Him might be saved." I was confident of God's unconditional love. It seemed logical to me that because I believed in a Biblical principle of celibacy, that I should not expect to be sexually active. I was not attracted to anyone of the same, or opposite sex. I had shut down my emotions and needs, to be available to the needs of others. I honestly believed I was no longer a lesbian and that all attractions were gone.

Imagine my surprise, shock, and horror when I realized I was wrong. I was a workshop leader at the Western States Women's conference for the Foursquare Church. I was teaching three weekends in a row, sharing my journey of healing and deliverance.

The first weekend, a woman from Lodi came up to speak with me after my class. She told me of a friend who would benefit from hearing my story. She wanted to know if she could bring that friend up the next weekend. I told her "sure," I'd be happy to counsel with her. We prayed together, and I forgot about the encounter.

The second week I was just beginning my seminar on "Healing the crumpled spirit," when I recognized the woman from the previous week. She came in and sat in the first row with the most beautiful woman I'd ever seen. This woman was about 5'10 with long thick black hair and was wearing a black leather outfit. Her eyes locked mine and a smile crept across her face.

My face flushed and burned with the heat of instant attraction. I was flustered in my presentation and for the next hour I avoided eye contact with her side of the room. I recounted my journey of healing by rote, but my brain was whirling with thoughts and emotions that I thought were gone.

I finished the talk, and then invited everyone to pray with me for healing of their bruised and broken spirits.

Silently I prayed, "Lord give me the words to help this woman in the front row."

The class ended, and the woman from the previous week made her way to the front, her friend in tow.

"Darlene, I want you to meet Des. She's the woman I told you about last week."

"Hello." I extended my hand. "I'm glad you could come to the conference."

I met her gaze, my face now bright red. *I hope she can't see how attracted I am to her. She's beautiful.*

She smiled. "I am too." She paused. "My friend tells me you do counseling and I wondered if I could make an appointment with you."

"Sure" I nodded and looked for a pen. "Let me give you my personal number. Just call and we can set something up at my church."

We talked for a few minutes and I suddenly became aware of several other women who wanted my attention. "Let's have a short prayer, and then call me during the week." The three of us held hands and I mumbled something about wisdom and strength in trusting Him."

When I opened my eyes, she was smiling. "I'll call this week." She gave my hand a gentle squeeze.

I turned to the group of women waiting to speak with me, and busied myself with selling copies of my books, and praying with each one who indicated a special need. My mind was spinning with the image of Des, and the fragrance of "Private Collection," that still lingered. Something was different and I desperately needed to pull myself together.

***

When Des called on Monday night, my heart was racing and my face flushed as I heard her voice. I spoke calmly. "It's good to hear from you. How are you?"

"I'm doing ok, but I have some issues I'd like to discuss with you." She paused.

"Could we make an appointment this week?"

"Let me check my calendar. When did you have in mind?"

"How about tomorrow night?" She hesitated. "I know you work, so I could make it about 7 P.M. It's only about an hours drive from Lodi."

"That will work for me." I gave her the address of the church. "I'll see you then."

I hung up the phone, grateful that she couldn't read my reaction. This was not my normal counseling appointment!

All that next day I wrestled with my attraction to Des, and my theology of freedom from same sex attraction. *I've got to face this situation in order to overcome these feelings. Once I've spent time with her, the feelings will go away.*

I arrived at the church at 6:30 and turned on the heat in my office. *What if she doesn't show up? Do I want her to show up? What's happening to me?*

The buzzer rang promptly at 7:00 and I opened the door and led her to my office.

"How was your drive?" I asked casually.

"It was ok. I actually came a couple hours ago and went out to dinner until our meeting. I wanted to miss the traffic."

"Oh, I'm sorry you had to wait. We could have made the appointment for an earlier time." *Why was I apologizing to her?*

"This is fine," she assured me. She took off her black leather jacket and sank down into the corner of the loveseat. She leaned back and crossed her legs, stretching out into the middle of my small office space.

"How tall are you?" I asked with a grin.

"About 5'10" She removed a Kleenex from her pocket and began to shred it as she talked. "I enjoyed your talk last Saturday."

I watched her face. She was beautiful; however her green eyes had a hint of sorrow and pain.

"How can I help you Des?" I paused. "Why don't you start talking about why you are here and give me some background information."

The one hour counseling session was still going strong at ll: 00 and a pile of shredded tissue lay on the floor beside the couch.

I had listened to her story of same sex attractions. She had been intrigued with sharing an apartment with a lesbian her first year of college. She had met other women through the years and had casual sexual relationships with them. She told me of her marriage to a man twenty five years her senior. He had been the choir director at her church when she was sixteen. She sang in the choir and he had flirted with her, until they developed a more personal relationship. John was twice divorced and was still with his current wife, but was deeply attracted to Des. Their affair went on for a couple of years, and eventually they married when she was nineteen. They had two sons, Nathan, fourteen and Phillip, thirteen. They were active teenagers, and completely occupied her life. She was unhappy in her marriage, but unsure of how she could change things. Her struggles were not new, but my desire to ease the pain in her heart was overwhelming.

"This is our first session Des. I'm willing to see you once a week; however we'll have to keep these sessions to an hour." I paused. "Why don't you drive over on Friday nights, and we can counsel before the support group meets. That way, you won't have to make this trip twice in a week, if you desire to start attending our support group."

"That sounds good to me." She smiled. "I really appreciate your time Darlene."

I held her gaze. "I've enjoyed getting to know you Des. Let's pray before you leave."

I reached over and took her hands, which were ice cold. I breathed a short sigh then prayed with her.

I felt a unique bonding of heart and spirit as we prayed together. Tears flowed down her cheeks, and a hard lump formed in my throat. This was not the usual counselee, and I was both scared and excited about what our sessions would discover. I wanted to help answer her questions about sexual orientation; however I wanted to be her friend. This attraction could be a dangerous combination for our counseling sessions.

The next Friday I received a call at my office about three o'clock.

"Hello Darlene. This is Des."

"Oh, hi." I murmured. "It's good to hear from you again."

"Well, I decided to come to group tonight, so I arrived early. I wondered if we might have an early dinner, do some counseling, and then attend the group."

I paused. "Sure, I think I could work that in. Where did you have in mind?"

"Well, I found a small Italian Restaurant up on Mission Blvd. It's called Bancherros. Do you know where it is?"

"Sure, I've been there before with church friends. How about 5:30?"

"That's fine. I'll make reservations and meet you there."

As soon as I hung up the phone, my stomach was in knots. *I shouldn't be socializing with a counselee. This could be misinterpreted if someone saw us. I really don't care. I can go out to dinner with anyone I please.*

My internal conversations carried on right up the driveway of the restaurant. I was looking forward to this dinner, and seeing Des again. She intrigued me and made me laugh. Her faith was of primary importance to her, and we were able to share scriptural concepts with a similar understanding due to our Evangelical backgrounds.

The dinner was pleasant. We were two friends sharing a meal. I could tell by the look in her eyes that my attraction to her was as strong as hers was to me. *I know I should refer to another counselor. I just don't want to do that!*

We went back to the church office after dinner and spent the next hour discussing topics of concern. Her marriage was over. She and her husband still shared the same home until they could agree on who would actually move. Her sons were responding to the conflicts of the marriage and their rebellion was a cause of much emotional pain. She had the full responsibility of caring for them, as her husband was absent emotionally, even when present in the house.

Des struggled with not only wanting a "best friend" with whom to share her life, but knowing that friend could never be her husband. She had developed a few close female friendships with women from church, but her attempts at "closeness" ended in guilt ridden emotions. Her longing to be loved and accepted totally by another human nagged at the core of her being. Her emotional life was on the edge of shattering, and she was looking for stability.

We talked of her leaving her husband, and raising the boys by herself. There were many hindrances to that solution. Her husband would not leave and she couldn't afford to have a place large enough for the three of them. Des was also concerned that her sons would want to stay with their father, as he was the more lenient of the two parents. A temporary solution was to move into a travel trailer beside their house to so she could have her own space, and yet have access to the full home kitchen and laundry facilities.

The hour passed quickly, and it was time for group to start in the back room.

Once again, we held hands, bowed our heads and prayed for wisdom and direction in her marriage, and in her life.

Paraklete, our Friday night support group, was open to men and women who were seeking a way out of the conflicts of unwanted sexual orientation. We held a short song session, a few scriptures were read then the men and women went to separate areas for in-depth discussions on the issues of the week. Many times, we focused on such topics as forgiveness, Christian love, and healthy friendships. Most of the group members were open to talking about these issues as they all seemed to struggle in these areas.

Each group member could share, or just sit and listen. Questions were asked, and answers given, based upon a biblical foundation. There was no condemnation of the clients, just encouragement for them to search the Bible for answers and to pray for God's strength.

Our group would then join with the men's group, and we would close in prayer.

Usually, we would adjourn to a restaurant for coffee and dessert and plan for the next meeting. I had individual appointments with group members and always available by phone for emergency situations.

I walked Des to her car after that first meeting. "You have a long drive home. Please be safe and call if there is anything I can do."

She looked up and smiled. "I will." She paused. "I'll call and let you know I'm home safe. Can we meet for dinner again next week"?

I grinned. "Sure. Let's do Mexican food. I know a good place right down the street." I watched her drive off into the darkness, mentally counting the days until I would see her again.

The days seemed to fly by, as I waited for Friday night, and dinner with Des. I was also planning a trip to Washington State to speak at an ex-gay conference in Seattle. My job at the insurance company kept me focused on reality, and all the things that had to be done before my trip north. Friday arrived and my heart was pounding as I drove to the Mexican restaurant after work. *What if she doesn't show up tonight?* My fears were unfounded. I saw her blue Cadillac as I pulled into the driveway. She was leaning against the door, watching for me.

We were led to a table in the back of the restaurant. I was happy, because it was a bit more private. "How has your week been going"? I queried.

"Things are going ok, I guess." She paused. "I've been thinking about you most of the week. I finished reading your book." She grinned. "You've led quite a life."

A huge lump grew in my throat as I tried to swallow a sip of diet coke. "I only wrote a small part of the events that make up my life." I looked directly at her sparkling green eyes. "Des, I've been thinking about you all week also." I paused. "I'm not so sure it's wise for us to meet for dinner before group each week."

A look of puzzlement crossed her face. "Why"?

I took a deep breath. "Well, I'm experiencing some strong feelings of attraction, at that's not a good thing for a counselor."

Her smile broadened. "I'm glad I'm not the only one!" She paused. "Darlene, I want to be your friend. I want to be able to talk to you, but I want to be your friend more than anything."

"Des, I don't think I can counsel you and also be your friend. We have to give this some deeper thought. I should refer you to another counselor, but I don't know anyone locally."

Our dinner came and we chatted about the lesson plan for the group meeting.

We finished eating then headed to the church. I was glad for a few minutes to try and sort out my emotions and my desire to help Des come to grips with her same sex attraction. She was a married woman. My heart was falling for this woman, and yet it didn't seem like the other affairs I had experienced during my life. Des was different. She was a Christian, and she was committed to finding God's will for her life, with or without her husband. She had been involved in several short relationships with women over the past few years, but they all ended with guilt after sexual contact. They were women from her church, and their families were involved with one another. Des' husband knew of a couple of the events, but he was involved in his own saga of adultery and was glad not to be pressured to be her best friend. He didn't want to spend a lot of time with her. Des' sons were young and didn't really understand the basis for the emotional distance between their parents. They didn't know of their fathers affairs, and thought their mother spent a too much time with her friends. The tension in the home was becoming unbearable for everyone.

The family life that was on the verge of ruin, and divorce was a common topic between Des and John. They both agreed that their marriage was on paper only, and that was soon to be addressed in a divorce court. The boys were experimenting with drugs and having their own first sexual experiments. Des was growing more and more depressed and felt isolated from those she should love the deepest. She was on the verge of suicide and had in fact written out her plan and left personal messages to her sons.

She had been estranged from her parents for several years since she ran off and married the choir director who was their age. He was a sexual predator in their eyes and they blamed him for Des not going on to college. They had never forgiven him, and had a difficult time forgiving Des. She ran into that relationship to escape the stringent home life and expectations of perfection from her mother.

These thoughts continued to bump around in my brain as I pulled into the church parking lot and greeted the first arrivals for group. My co-director, Daphne, was waiting for me at the door. We shared a home together, and although she was straight, she acted like my "non-sexual" wife.

"Why didn't you come home after work?" She whined. "I had dinner ready for you."

"Sorry," I muttered. "I went out to dinner with a friend."

"Who"? She questioned.

"I don't have to fill you in on all my dinner partners." I shot back. "It was just a friend."

She glanced at Des walking into the church. "Did you go out with her"?

She paused. "You did, didn't you? I can't believe you would risk your ministry to have dinner with a counselee alone."

"Let it be, Daphne. I'm a big girl and can take care of myself."

I went to my office and got the papers for the group meeting. *That woman drives me crazy!* I walked back to the fellowship hall where everyone had gathered. Daphne took her place at the piano and glared at me. She led us in several worship songs and we gathered around the table for discussion with the men and women together. We shared events from the week and read each of the 12 steps from the Homosexual Anonymous materials. We used several books based upon a 12 Step recovery from sexual addiction. We took prayer requests, then Mark, the men's group leader took the men to another part of the church for group discussion, and I led the women's discussion.

"As most of you know, I will be leaving for Seattle next week and will not be here for our meeting. I've asked Sandy to lead the group, as both Daphne and I will be at the conference. I glanced at Des. "If any of you need to call me, please call my cell phone. I'll keep in touch that way."

An hour later the men rejoined the group and we ended in prayer. I walked to the parking lot with several of the women. Des hung back so that she could talk privately.

"I'll call you when I'm home." She smiled. "We need to finish that conversation from the restaurant."

I nodded. "I'll wait up until I hear from you."

I drove home and went into my room, shutting the bedroom door so that Daphne would not initiate any conversations. She came bursting through the door as soon as she arrived home.

"What's going on between you and Des?" She was screaming her accusation.

"Nothing," I replied. "We're just spending extra time counseling privately.

"You know it's not right to counsel without an accountability person in the area."

"I'm a big girl and can take care of myself, Daphne. You don't have to be present every time I'm talking with a client." I paused. "Besides, she is becoming more of a friend than a counselee."

"You can't be friends with someone struggling with homosexuality," she blurted. "You're just asking for trouble."

"She is a Christian woman; she's married and has some issues to work through. I can be friends with anyone. I don't have to limit my relationships to someone who has never had a queer thought!" I walked to the door and motioned for Daphne to leave. "I need to make some calls and I'd like privacy please."

I shut the door then picked up the phone. I needed to talk with a friend in Chicago who was also in ministry. I dialed her number and took a deep breath, hoping she was still up at this late hour.

"Hello" Judy came on the line.

"Hi, friend. How are things in Chicago"? I tried to sound casual.

"Not too bad. I'm keeping busy." She paused. "What's so important that you are calling me at midnight on a Friday night"?

"Well, I just needed someone to talk with, and you are about the only one I can trust." I hesitated. "I think I am about to crash and burn."

"What's going on"? She questioned. I now had her full attention.

"I met this woman that I am very attracted to sexually, mentally, emotionally and spiritually. She is the woman I have looked for all my life and I've only known her a couple of weeks." I blurted out the story of our meeting and how I hadn't been able to get Des off my mind since that day.

Judy listened to the story. "It's all just raging hormones and it will pass. We all deal with attractions from time to time." She paused. "Find her another counselor."

"That's not the answer, Judy. I've been praying about this and I feel like God brought her into my life. I'm ready to give up ministry to share my life with her."

"You've made that decision already"?

"Yes and I haven't even told her." I ventured another thought. "This is more than sexual attraction. I know what we teach at Exodus, and I know all the emotional dependency theories. I know how we apply Scripture to the situations that we counsel every day. I don't have it all figured out yet, but I am convinced that God is in this relationship and that perhaps all the answers I thought I had are merely a starting place for new questions.

I rambled on for a few minutes. "I have just one more question. Will you still be my friend if I give up ministry and pursue this relationship?"

She didn't even hesitate. "Darlene, I will always be your friend. I just want you to pray about this and make sure you want to leave ministry and go through all the opposition that you will receive from Exodus and your church. Have you thought about what will happen with your books"?

"No, I am just trying to be true to my heart." I hesitated. "I don't know what my future holds. I still have a lot of scheduled speaking engagements and television appearances and want to fulfill my commitments. I wanted to know if my world falls apart that I have one friend that will be there for me to talk with at midnight"!

"You can call anytime Darlene. I won't reject you, and neither will Jesus."

"When I was in college, that's what the Dean of Women always told me. Mrs. Hollowell has been like a mother to me for over thirty years, so I know I have at least three people in my corner!" I chuckled. "I need to let you go. Des will be calling in a few minutes."

"I'll call you in a few days to see how things are going."

"That sounds good. You better make it a week. I'm going to Seattle to speak at that conference. I won't make any rash decisions until then." I chuckled. "I'll be alright if I can keep Daphne from blabbing her suspicions to the world."

I hung up and the phone rang instantly. "Hi" I whispered as if to a lover. "I've been waiting for your call."

She laughed. "Not too patiently. I've been calling for the last ten minutes."

"Oh, well, I was talking with a friend in Chicago."

"You are a popular lady, even at this late hour." Her voice thrilled my soul

"Well, someone has to do it. Might as well be me." I tried to lighten up the conversation. "I'm glad you made it home with no problems."

"Darlene, the only problem I have is being incredibly attracted to you." Her voice was low and seductive. "I know you won't understand this, but I've been praying for you and trying to sort out my feelings. I won't go to another counselor. I believe that God has brought our lives together for a purpose and that we need to find out what that purpose is. I've read the material from group and I know that you think homosexuality is a sin, but I don't find that in the Scripture. I'd like to spend time looking at what the Bible really says, and if it is a sin, then why would God give us these feelings"?

I was blown away emotionally. *Had I been that transparent that she knew what I was feeling about our relationship? What is going on?*

"Des, I seem to have more questions than answers when it comes to knowing why God does anything these days. I am scared to death of my feelings for you, and I shouldn't even be telling you that, because all my teaching says to run like hell. I'm willing to talk with you and pray about what we should actually be doing in regards to counseling. I leave for a week, and when I'm back, we can reschedule some time together."

"You're not going to run away from me, are you"? Her voice was filled with mirth.

"No, I'm not running away. We need some space to figure out where this is going. Let's meet a week from Monday at my office at the church"?

"I'll be there." Her voice faded to a low murmur. "I feel in my soul as if we have known each other all our lives, Darlene. I can't explain how that is, but I know that another week will not make any difference in how I feel"

We talked until about three in the morning. I was physically and emotionally exhausted when we hung up the phone. This relationship was beyond my control. I felt as if the past ten years of emotional and sexual abstinence had left me numb, and not "healed." I fell asleep that night with a vision of my life as an incomplete puzzle, and the face of Des was the final puzzle piece being snapped into place.

The next week was filled with doing ministry as usual. I taught at the conference, did interviews and gave all the standard answers to questions on freedom from homosexuality. My heart was split from my brain, and I prayed that the inconsistency did not reveal itself. I dared not speak of the conflict. I chuckled to myself on more than one occasion. *If I called Exodus to talk about my feelings they would refer me to* **me** *for counseling!*

Late one night in Seattle after the conference, I found a few minutes to make a call .The phone rang twice.

"Hello" Des' voice was an oasis in the desert of my conflict.

"Hi. It's just me. I wanted to check in and see how you were doing."

"I've been thinking of you all day. I was praying that God would give you wisdom and insight as you speak at the conference. How are you doing?" Her tone was one of concern.

"I'm still working on things in my brain." I chuckled. "When I was taking literature in college, I learned a little poem. It states: I put my hand upon my heart and vowed that we would never part. I wonder what I might have said, if I had laid it on my head! I don't remember who wrote it, but it's true."

She laughed. "Don't be afraid of your emotions Darlene. God gave them to you along with your brain."

"Right." I paused. "Well, I need to go. I just wanted you to know I was thinking about you and looking forward to our session on Monday."

"I'll be there at seven." she continued. "Darlene, don't take this wrong, but I love you."

"We'll talk about that on Monday," I sputtered. "I have to go now."

The rest of the week was filled with events and interviews that I can't even remember. I spent one day visiting Mrs. Hollowell, my former college dean. I wanted so much to talk with her and share my story about Des. I knew she would still love and accept me, but I needed to figure this out on my own before I tried to explain it to the world.

Daphne watched me like a hawk, but didn't ask any questions, and seemed happy that I was not in contact with anyone from our group, especially Des. I still needed time to mull over the events of the previous two weeks. I really hadn't done anything that would remove me from ministry. It was all a raging turbulence within my soul. It occurred to me the last night of our "vacation" that I was tired of being in the spotlight all the time. I was tired of always being available to the world, and never available to the little Darlene who lived inside me. That night, I fell asleep with thoughts of my Heavenly Father holding me on His lap and whispering, "I will never let evil harm you. You are my beloved daughter, and everything I give you is good." I slept sound, and for the first time in weeks, I wasn't afraid of what the future would bring.

On Monday, I returned to work. After so many years in the insurance business, I could do my job and not have to expend much energy. My thoughts were on the meeting with Des at seven. I called Daphne and told her I would be working late then meeting a client at the Church.

She was hesitant. "Do you need me to be there? I can practice piano in the sanctuary."

"No." I didn't address her unasked question. "I will make sure the door to my office is open."

I arrived fifteen minutes early and unlocked the church. I was the assistant pastor, so had full access to the church even after hours. I went to the kitchen and made a pot of coffee.

I heard a car drive into the parking lot and went to the door. My heart was pounding as I watched this five foot ten woman with black hair and black leather jacket emerge from the vehicle. *God, she's beautiful.* I gulped hard and managed to squeak out a greeting.

"How was the traffic"?

"Not too bad actually," she grinned. "I came early and had a bite to eat at the Italian restaurant." She brushed by me as I held the door, then stopped and gave me a quick hug. "It's good to see you again."

"You too." I stepped away. "Do you want some coffee"?

"That would be nice." She grinned. "I had a glass of wine with dinner, so coffee will help keep me awake."

I walked to the kitchen and poured two cups. "Do you take anything"?

"Just milk." She opened the refrigerator and took out the milk. "How about you"?

"Just black." I responded.

I motioned for her to follow me to my office at the front of the church. I had one recliner and a loveseat, along with my desk and bookshelf in a tiny room about ten feet square.

"Sit where you are the most comfortable." I suggested.

She chose the recliner. I curled up on the loveseat and picked up a pad and pen. "Do you mind if I take notes"?

"No" She cocked her head to one side. "I'm glad that you want to remember what we talk about."

It was ten o'clock when I became aware of the time. Our conversation had covered her life for the past thirty nine years. She openly spoke of her marriage and her husband's affairs, her children and her affairs with a few women from her church. We talked about how her commitment was first to God, then to her family, and how her faith gave her a deep understanding of God's grace. I had avoided talking about "us" or where the relationship might be headed.

She looked directly into my eyes. "Can we pray"?

"Of course." I was surprised that she would think we wouldn't invite God into our time together.

In one gliding movement, she was out of her chair and knelt in front of me. Our eyes were at the same level. She slipped her hands into mine and began to talk with God, just as we had been in conversation. I kept my eyes open and watched her face, as she poured out her heart of thankfulness for finding a place of safety. I was about to pray when she opened her eyes and slipped her arms around my neck. Our lips met in a tender kiss.

My heart and brain were exploding. *I should pull away.* I slipped my arms around her and pulled her to me, without hesitation. *This is what I have longed for all my life. I experienced completeness in bonding and in that moment, I knew in my soul that Des and I were meant to be together.* I couldn't explain it, but I knew it was right.

We held the embrace for what seemed like hours. Actuality, only a few minutes had passed.

"What will happen next"? She questioned.

"I don't know." I whispered. "We will need to take things one step at a time."

She stood to her feet, and towered over me by several inches.

"Come with me." I took her hand and walked to the front of the church. There were several steps leading to the platform. I walked up two of them then turned around and faced her. Once again we were at eye level.

I cupped her face in my hands and kissed her softly. "All that we are, all that we will be, I commit myself to you Des, for now and for the future. I can't explain it, but I know that God has brought our lives together." I stepped up another step and bent down and kissed her again. "Now you know what it's like to kiss someone taller than you"! I laughed aloud. "I'm not sure how we got here…but we'll figure it out"!

It was almost midnight. "Why don't you call your husband and tell him you're spending the night with friends in Hayward? It's too late for you to drive over an hour home tonight. You can sleep on my couch."

"I already told him I wouldn't be home tonight. I knew we would have a lot to talk about and I didn't want to rush our conversation."

We drove to my place, and I gave her my bed and I slept on the couch. I wasn't ready to make love with Des until I knew for sure, that this was more than raging hormones.

How would God convince me that my sexuality was a gift, not a curse?

CHAPTER TWO
GOD IS FAITHFUL EVEN WHEN ORGANIZED MINISTRY IS REMOVED.

The entire month of November was spent going through the scriptures with Des and long discussions about the grace of God. I had a friend who just graduated from seminary and I decided to confide in her. Dianne was heterosexual, and had never passed judgment on my life. She was knowledgeable in the Hebrew and Greek scriptures, so we planned several study sessions to look at the sections that discussed homosexuality.

I was intrigued to discover that the word translated homosexuality, was not in the early texts. There were variations that meant "soft" or "effeminate" but it was in the 1940's that the translations began to insert homosexual, in the place of less specific terms. It was also apparent that Jesus never spoke to the issue of homosexuality in any red letter edition that I could find. I read through the Gospels several times, then through Paul's epistles and asked the Lord for insights into how my Christian life could be modeled after His own. This was not my first time of studying the scripture. I had spent years in Bible College preparing myself for ministry. I had known others who had struggled with homosexuality and had been in therapy for years. The first deeply emotional relationship I had experienced in college had led to acting out sexually. My life had been devastated when Linda had committed suicide due to her inability to handle the condemnation from her church and the pressure from her family. I was just seventeen and my experience with loving and being loved, then having that torn away in a moment of time, had deeply impacted how I viewed the Bible. I was shown scriptures to support how homosexual behavior was a sin. I felt like God had abandoned me much like my own father had abandoned me when my parents were divorced. My heart longed for acceptance from a relationship with Jesus, but I felt separated because my heart had also been awakened to same sex attraction. That conflict continued all my life, and was the basis for why I had become involved in ex-gay ministry.

It dawned on me that what I had been doing, as was every other ex-gay ministry, was to approach the scripture with the premise that homosexuality was sin. Every scripture was then viewed in that light, and interpretation was revealed on that faulty premises. If, as we taught, homosexuality was a choice, then we could identify it as sin. Choice was always something you could alter with the correct incentives. Sexual orientation had not been proven to be genetic. It must be a result of many choices made throughout the life of the individual. All of the teaching and sermons that I had embraced for so many years made the same assumption. *What if I was wrong? What if Exodus was wrong? What if the scriptures didn't express the conviction that homosexuality was a sin? What if everyone who said they spoke for God on this topic was in fact speaking from their own limited view of sexuality and grace?*

Another thing bothered me. Many of those whom I counseled, those I knew from Exodus, and in my most honest moments with myself, even I still longed for same sex bonding. I made the choice for many years not to act upon the feelings, and that was my only choice. I couldn't change the feelings at the core of my being, because they were never meant to be changed. God had created me with a sexual orientation that was to be celebrated, not healed! The more I searched the Scriptures, the more sense it made that we were trying to give back a gift to God that He could never take back. This meant that all the therapy and deliverance in the world could not change me or anyone who was gifted with a homosexual orientation. My theology, ministry and writing have been an unintentional deception as I tried to guide those with conflicted sexuality into a wholeness they could never experience. Once again, I was devastated by my efforts to help others, only to hear story after story of continued agony and despair. I didn't have the answer for them because I had been asking the wrong questions.

Des and I spent hours discussing these revelations and what it meant to be truly Christian and Gay. How did we live a Christian lifestyle, and model grace and acceptance of all of God's children?

I had been writing and speaking and teaching for over ten years about the choices we make to be homosexual. Now, there was no way to un-ring the bell. I was still directing an ex-gay ministry, as well as being the assistant pastor at church and continued to write and appear on television shows around the country. How could I just fade away? More importantly, could I leave the limelight of ministry and be content to live out my life with this woman God had brought into my life? What if she were really a trap from Satan? I would be an outcast once I openly reversed my teaching of sexual orientation and stepped down from ministry.

There seemed to be no easy way to communicate my new understanding of the Scripture. I could not continue to teach what I had believed for so long. I fell on my knees and cried out to God for direction and wisdom. I had to be true to myself, whether or not Des would commit to me. This was only 6 weeks after our first meeting at the women's conference in October. I had not yet entered into a sexual relationship with Des for fear that my entire life would fall apart. We also needed to talk about the moral issue of adultery.

I lived for the weekends. Des would arrive early on Friday and we would go to dinner. We would go to the church and talk before the group meeting. Our relationship was very intense, and I knew it was only a matter of time before someone in the group would notice, and confront us. We made several decisions in those early weeks. I would not accept any more speaking engagements. I would attend the Exodus conference in Kentucky and teach the classes I was committed to teach. I planned to approach Mark, who directed the men's group and Sandra, who assisted me in leading the women; and secure a commitment of confidentiality from them. I wanted to share what was happening with Des and me. I was willing to turn the group over to their leadership in order to still provide a place for healing for the men and women who attended our group. As the conference went on, it seemed better to wait until we were back in Hayward to share the news with them.

I wasn't sure what I would do about my position in the church. It would be easier to explain away my absence from Paraklete than to stop being the assistant pastor. We agreed to pray about that, and just continue with ministry.

After group on Friday night, I would follow Des to Lodi and spend the weekend at her home in the spare bedroom. Her husband was seldom home, and her boys were almost always with friends. We enjoyed long walks in the woods, stolen kisses and talking about the Scripture. Des was convinced that we were all God's children and that nothing could separate us from His love. All sin was forgiven by the blood of Jesus at Calvary. Her faith was simple, but her family life was complicated.

My presence each weekend had put more stress on their already fragile marriage. John had long ago abdicated his position as her husband in the Biblical sense. She didn't feel that she would be committing adultery as their marriage had been a sham for many years. Des talked about filing for divorce and taking care of some legal matters that had long plagued their finances. She had a talk with him and asked him for a divorce, and to move from the house and leave it for her and the boys. He agreed to a divorce, but refused to leave the house. Des could continue to sleep in the trailer along side of the house if she didn't want to share his bedroom.

We spent one weekend fixing the trailer to make it a more permanent location. It was just a few steps to the house, so she had use of the kitchen and bathrooms. . I hooked up a phone so that she would be able to call me if something happened. I had invited her to move into my place, but she wanted to stay near the boys until they were out of school. That would be at least four years. I told her I would wait as long as we needed to, and that God would give us the direction for our lives. I continued to spend each weekend with her, and my absence from my church was obvious. I told Daphne that she needed to find another place to live, and that I would help her do that soon.

The weeks passed quickly, and the more time Des and I spent together, the more convinced I was that this was a forever relationship. She was still sleeping in the travel trailer, and was feeling the stress on Nathan and Phillip as they acted out their frustrations and hurt over the emotional separation of their parents. They told Des that they wanted to stay with their father, and she was free to leave. We began to make plans to have that happen, and to file the paperwork for her divorce.

Shortly after I finished my commitment to speak at Exodus I called a meeting and spoke to my two group leaders; Mark and Sandra. . They were shocked, and told me they would not let me bow out quietly. Mark went to Exodus and asked that I be removed from the referral status and any leadership. My pastor was part of my executive board, so he was also notified. I was called into the office and confronted with my relationship with Des. I was given the alternative of never seeing her again, or turning in my resignation as assistant pastor of the church. I pulled it from my pocket and handed it to the pastor.

"I figured that you would leave me no other choice." I said quietly. "I am committed to following the leading of the Lord, and although we disagree about what the Bible says about homosexuality, I know that He is directing my path."

"We will pray for you Darlene, and I'll notify headquarters that you are resigning to deal with moral issues."

I looked him square in the eyes. "I know one thing pastor, The Foursquare church didn't call me to preach. My call came from God many years ago, and He never takes away His gifts or calling." I stood and walked toward the door in his office. "I'll miss the people here, but I have no regrets."

That night at the Paraklete meeting, I addressed the group. "This will be the last meeting to be held at this church, or under the title of Paraklete. I wanted Mark and Sandra to continue the group, but Mark has made it impossible for me to leave quietly. He will be starting another group at the Baptist Church, and you can obtain details from him. Des and I believe that God has brought our lives together and we are going to follow His leading. I'm saddened that this will end and I want you all to know that we will love and pray for you."

Daphne was crying as were several others in the group. I spoke softly. "Jesus will continue to meet your needs. You need to be strong in your faith. Don't look at me as a failure of healing. I am more whole now than I have ever been. If any of you wish to contact me privately, I am leaving you copies of my resignation letter and it has my number at home."

I stood at the end of the table and took Des' hand. "This meeting is over. I need for you to leave so that I can close the church and empty my office." Tears trickled down my cheeks. This was the end of ministry and I had no idea what God had in mind for us to do with the rest of our lives.

Des and I went back to my house that night. Daphne had located a small mobile home in town and we had helped her finance it. Tonight there would be no need to sneak kisses or withhold hugs. Tonight we were on the edge of changes greater than we could comprehend. Tonight was a time for prayer and lots of silence as we relived the past couple of days.

Early the next morning, the ringing phone shattered my isolation from the world. I picked it up slowly. "Hello, this is Darlene".

"Darlene, this is Jane at Chosen Books. Do you have time to talk"?

"Of course, I've always got time for my publisher."

"Well, that's what I need to talk about." She paused. "I received a call today with information that you have gone back to the lifestyle. I'm calling to ask if it's true."

"That didn't take long," I blurted. "I could debate what going back to the lifestyle means, but I won't. I believe that God has brought a woman into my life and I intend to spend the rest of my life with her. I guess you would consider that a reversal of the message of my books."

"I'm sorry to hear that, Darlene. We will be pulling your books from our list and our professional relationship will end. I want you to know that I love you and care about what you are doing. I don't know how this happened, but if you ever want to talk, I am here."

"Jane," I began. "It would take a long time to tell you how this journey has come full circle to where it is today. I know your theology, and I know that I've disappointed many people. I also know in the depths of my soul that Jesus is my Lord and Savior and He is leading me in this path."

"I am very disappointed. You are a great writer and a good person. I think you are making a huge mistake. You will be receiving an official letter terminating our contract. I will be praying for you." She hung up.

I turned to Des. "Well, no church, no books, no ministry!" I laughed. "Let's go to Hawaii." I walked over and put my arms around her. "Are you sure you want to live with this has-been preacher?"

"Darlene," she held me even closer. "You are not and never will be a has-been preacher. God will continue to open doors for you to reach people who are hurting. I don't know how, or where, but He isn't finished with you by a long shot!"

Gentle tears erupted into convulsive sobs. "I'm not sure I know who or what I am without ministry! I've been doing this so long my identity is what I do, not what I feel."

"God will give us direction, honey." She pulled back and looked into my eyes. "No matter what happens, we know that God brought us together for a purpose, and we will find that purpose together"!

I wish I could say that was the last time we cried together and that God brought new direction. Each of us was at the crossroads of leaving our known past behind and stepping out to an unknown future. Des left her marriage with her clothes and a few personal items. Her sons were angry and rebellious. Her husband was indifferent. Her church friends cut her off from all contact and she was the talk of her small town. Everyone knew that she was living with a lesbian lover, and her husband soaked up the sympathy as the jilted husband.

I was angry and wanted to take out an ad in the local paper to set the record straight. Des didn't care so much about her husband, but her boys broke her heart. She prayed for them daily and tried to keep in contact. Sometimes weeks went by with no word from them, and the tears could not wash away the pain. Her dreams were often tormented with fears of injury to her sons. She was powerless to change their rejection of her in those early months.

Des did the only thing she knew to do. She sent cards and letters and called to leave messages. She told her sons that she loved them and would be there for them. She offered to come back home if they wanted her to be there. Her husband was seeing other women as he was now free to date.

I comforted her often, and together we cried and prayed that God would bring reconciliation with her sons. Her loss was similar to the loss of my ministry family, and we knew that neither of these situations would ever be as they had been in the past.

I continued to receive calls from across the country from people who read my book and wanted to talk to someone who had been "healed" from homosexuality. I referred most calls to different ministries in their local areas.

Des confronted me after one such call. "Why don't you tell the callers how God is working in your life now"?

"You mean just say I'm now living with my lesbian lover"?

"Yes, but you could tell them about the process of how you and I have sought God and the insights we have gained in the Scriptures." She walked across the room and put her arms around me. "I'm not going to live in a spiritual closet, and neither are you."

I nodded. "You are right about that, Des. I'm not ashamed of you or the path that God is directing for our lives. The next call I receive from someone looking for help, will get the full truth"!

I had my opportunity two days later. I was watching television and the phone rang. Des picked it up. "Hello" She listened for a moment. "She's right here. Just a moment and I'll put Darlene on the line." She handed the phone to me with a smile. "This person just finished reading your book and wants to talk with you."

I took a deep breath and said a silent prayer for wisdom. "This is Darlene Bogle"

An excited voice came across the line. "I can't believe I'm really speaking to you. I just finished reading your book of <u>Long Road to Love.</u>" There was a pause. "So much of your book could be my story. I'm a Christian and have tried for so many years to get over the feelings of attraction for women. I've not been acting out, but I struggle all the time with wanting a woman's love. I pray and read my Bible all the time, but the feelings are still there. How long did it take for you not to have those feelings"?

The moment of truth was here. "You may be surprised by what I'm going to tell you, but you need to know the truth." I paused, and then continued. "I spent several years keeping myself so busy that I had no time to feel anything, and I had no attractions to women or men. I committed myself to prayer and Bible reading, just as you indicated. I knew I loved God and that He loved me. The feelings of attraction for women are part of your sexual orientation and will never go away. God created us as sexual beings with the capacity to love and express love."

"But homosexuality is a sin"! She protested.

"Is it"? I questioned. "I think it is important to understand that God cannot take away His gifts. Sexuality is God's gift to us. I think that He wants us to use that gift responsibly, but I don't think it is a correct understanding of Scripture to say that homosexuality is sin. There is a lot of theology that is misunderstood by well intended spiritual leaders. I recommend that you purpose to seek God and deepen your relationship with Him. Don't be so concerned about what you are feeling in being attracted to women."

"Wow. I didn't expect to hear that from you after reading your book."

"God has continued to lead me on this journey. Just because my book ended, my spiritual growth has continued and my understanding of my own sexuality and God's acceptance of my sexual orientation is an ongoing process."

"So, does that mean you are gay now"? She questioned.

"What is means for me is that I am a Christian, with a homosexual orientation. I chose not to act on it for several years, and when I wrote my books, I assumed that meant that I was no longer gay. What God has been revealing to me is that He has created me with my sexual orientation, and I cannot change what is a part of me. He wants for me to keep Him first in my life, and let my sexuality take care of itself."

"There are so many preachers who say it's a sin. How do you answer them"?

"There are lots of things that are sin. Hatred and bigotry and lies are just a few. Christ died for all sin, and as a Christian, I believe that if loving someone of the same sex were a sin, then Christ has already paid the price for that sin. However, if you read the New Testament, you will not find one statement from Christ about homosexuality." I paused. "I have purposed in my heart to not argue with those who disagree with my understanding of the Scripture, but to love my brothers and sisters in Christ, and to walk in forgiveness toward those who choose to condemn me."

The voice on the line was silent.

"Are you still there"? I asked quietly.

"Yes," she paused. "Thank you for telling me the truth about how you understand your journey at this time in your life. I'm not sure I'm there yet. I've been told it's a sin for so long that it's hard to hear and believe something different."

"I understand that. What I'd really like for you to do is quit listening to what people tell you and open your Bible. Ask God to reveal His heart to you in a new and deeper way. Don't just read the verses that have to deal with sexuality, but read entire books at one sitting. The Bible says that the Holy Spirit is our teacher, so ask Him to instruct you in truth!"

"I'll do that," she promised.

"Please do one more thing. Give me a call in a few months and let me know what you are learning from the Heart of God. I'll be praying that the God of all truth will lead you into His truth, even if it is different that anything you've ever heard."

I hung up the phone, and Des came over and gave me a hug. "That took a lot of courage, but you did well." She paused. "You gave her more hope than she has ever heard from the pulpit "

"It's just so scary to tell someone who has just finished reading my book that God is not finished with me either. I thought I had all the answers when that book came off the press. Now I'm realizing I have a hundred questions, and I'm still looking for answers."

"We'll find them together, Darlene." She sat on the couch next to me and took my hand. "If we are living in sin, then God will reveal it to us. If our desire and commitment is to love God with all our heart and follow the intent of His Word to us, then He will not lead us astray."

"I believe that with all my heart." I chuckled. "It's just my brain that wants to keep slipping back into the same responses that I've been giving for ten years"!

We prayed together that day, as we did everyday, asking for great wisdom and courage to show God's love to every person that came our way. I discovered as with most of my prayers, it was easier to ask God for wisdom and love than it was to live out in my life.

I received at least one phone call a week from someone who had just finished reading my book or who had seen me on a television program. I wasn't always bold in proclaiming my new journey. It seemed especially difficult when a parent would call and be so distraught over their son or daughters homosexuality, and want me to give the magic words to fix them. I wanted to provide encouragement and most often told them to just love their children and pray for them. I emphasized that they were God's children first and He was able to deal with them and bring them to wholeness. I was a chicken to say "God created them as gay and lesbian children, so just love and accept them and help them to celebrate their uniqueness." I have wished many times over the years that I had learned to tell the whole truth when someone called with those types of questions.

Des and my personal spiritual journey took on its own life. We initially received calls from those in the support group, asking us to repent and come back to God.

My response was "How can I come back to God when I've never left Him, and He has never left me"? I would quote the appropriate, "I will never leave or forsake you verse" from Hebrews 13:5.

I would ask, "How can I repent, which means to 'turn from' something that is a part of who I am? I repent of my attitude of anger and resentment that creeps in when I receive a call from someone who tells me they are speaking for God and suggest that I am incapable of hearing from Him directly." At that point, I would pause and before they could respond, I would continue. "The Bible tells me that I should not let bitterness take root, which will defile many, so I choose to forgive you for trying to play Holy Spirit in my life and convict me of sin."

The conversations would come to an end, and after a few weeks, we were not receiving any further communication from our former "friends" in the group. Another fact that surprised us was that of all the ministry friends I had been involved with at Exodus International, only a handful called to say they were praying for us. It was as if they didn't know what to say, and chose not to have any involvement.

As my exodus from Exodus became known throughout the organization, there was a surprising reaction from several leaders and members. I would receive a call, and when they identified themselves, I expected to be reproved for my relationship with Des. I was shocked when I heard on several occasions, the reason for the call.

It went something like this. "Darlene, you are the only person I can talk with that will not "out" me to Exodus. I have struggled with my feelings of attraction for women, (or men) for a long time, but there is no one I can share this struggle with who would not make me leave Exodus. I love the ministry and being able to help people. I respect the fact that you are following your heart and allowing God to bring you a Christian woman to share your life. I wish I had your courage."

The first time I received such a call I was in shock. *I'm not the only one who didn't get healed by repeating the mantra over and over!* I would listen to their story, and give my word that I would never "out" them to Exodus or anyone else. It was their journey to travel and God would lead them as He had me. I became a pastor and counselor to many Exodus leaders, when they felt they had no one else to turn to for counsel. Many of them stayed in ministry, and some of them left for a variety of reasons, and found life partners without Exodus ever being aware of their struggle.

Some of the leaders were caught in sexual situations, and were dismissed from ministry. My heart broke each time I would hear of a situation, and I would try to contact the leader to provide encouragement. When I was unable to make contact, Des and I would add their name to a growing list of daily prayer requests.

The weeks quickly became months, and Des and I were without a place to fellowship on Sunday mornings. We would read the Bible and pray together often, but our hearts longed for a place to worship. We visited several churches in our local area that were large enough that we could remain invisible. We joined in the worship time, and sat through sermons that invariably touched on the "sin" of homosexuality. We would look for another church, longing for a place to worship as a couple.

We met a lesbian couple in the mobile home park where we lived. They invited us to the Lutheran Church in Newark, California. We were told it was a "Reconciled in Christ" church and that we would be welcomed as a gay couple.

Our first Sunday was interesting. As we drove into the parking lot I recognized the building. I had been a speaker at a seminar a few years earlier when the church was debating the question of homosexuality, and whether to become a reconciled church. I turned to Des.

"I hope that no one remembers me from when I was on the other side of the gay issue."

"It won't make any difference now Darlene. You're on the right side of the issue and if they don't welcome us, we'll keep looking for the right church." She squeezed my hand. "Let's go see how the Lutherans receive gay people."

As we walked through the front door, we were greeted by a lesbian couple who were active in the church. We saw our new friends from the mobile home park and joined them in the pew. The liturgy of the service was strange, and more formal than Des' Baptist experience and my Charismatic background.

What was comfortable was the instant acceptance we experienced from the heterosexual couples in the congregation. We were warmly embraced during the welcoming time and several women did come up and acknowledge that they remembered me from the time I had spoken on behalf of Exodus several years earlier. They had no hesitation with receiving Des and I as a couple and didn't ask how it was that I was in a lesbian relationship. We held hands during most of the service. We went joyfully to receive communion from the elders at the end of the service.

We talked on the way home about feeling for the first time that God was making a public stamp of approval on our love. The worship songs were not what we were used to experiencing, however we could always attend a more lively church in the evenings and leave after the song service. We were ready to commit ourselves for six months to this church and see where God might lead in terms of ministry.

The minister was a younger man in his late thirties. Howard was outgoing, and his sermons were based upon social justice and living one's faith through meeting the needs of the homeless. He didn't quote lengthy sections of scripture or invite anyone to receive Jesus as Lord and Savior. Des was uncomfortable that Howard didn't seem to preach a familiar Gospel.

"Let's go out to lunch with him, or invite him to the house for a talk if it makes you so uneasy," I offered. "I'm sure that he meets with new visitors to his church."

That next week he agreed to drop over on a Thursday night. Des was ready with a lot of questions about the Lutheran faith and what they actually believed.

Howard patiently went through the tenants of faith, and explained how each was relevant in our Christian walk.

"There's something I don't understand," she said. "It all looks good on paper, but I don't hear you preaching Christ or Salvation."

"Really"! Howard was shocked. "I think Christ is in every sermon I preach."

"I just don't hear that." Des responded.

"Des, you don't have to preach hell fire and damnation with a plan of salvation each Sunday. Christ walked through life speaking against injustice, feeding the poor and praying for the sick and rejected. He told us to be followers and to go out and do the things that He did while on earth. How is that not preaching Christ"?

She laughed. "When you put it that way, I see how Christ is in your sermons. I'm just used to it being more direct."

Howard responded softly. "I'm sure that the Spirit's job is to reveal Christ to His people, and the words that I speak on Sunday are just one vehicle of representing the Christ nature. We need to do more, speak less, in my opinion."

We prayed together before Howard left, and Des was satisfied with his answers. She called after him as he went down the stairs. "I'm going to be listening for Jesus on Sunday"!

"Great." He called back. "You'll find Him walking through every illustration."

We became more comfortable with the liturgy as time went on, and Howard began to involve us in the service. We joined the church, and became the prayer counselors after each service. Des joined the choir and talked me into joining also, so that we could be together. Within months, I was asked to be on the board of elders and work with the organization of the church. I was allowed to serve communion on Sundays, and even allowed to preach one Sunday, although I was not a licensed Lutheran minister. Des and I became involved in teaching the adult Sunday School class, and we settled down into the family fabric of church structure.

God seemed to be restoring aspects of ministry that I thought were gone forever.

Des and I had many long discussions about what type of ministry we would become involved with in the local church. On one occasion, she began to share her fears at my being such a public figure.

"Darlene, I want you to make a promise to me." Her tone was very serious.

"Sure honey. What is it"? I questioned.

"I want you to promise me that you will not do any writing on being ex-gay, or on our life together. I don't want anything in the public media that might be seen by my family."

I took her hands in mine. "Des, I was a voice for the ex gay movement for a lot of years. My life was not my own to go on non- ministry vacations, or even be free from phone counseling. I don't want to be in that position again. I want to be supportive of Gay rights, but will not do it by writing or speaking on national television. Our life and time is too special to me to get out in the public again. I promise you I will not do any writing for publication or go on any more speaking circuits."

"This is really important to me, Darlene. My family would totally disown me if they found out that you and I are a gay couple. I don't trust John or the boys either to not say anything to my parents. Someday, it won't make any difference, but right now, it does. I know how important writing is to you, and God has gifted you, but I need your word that you really will not be out there fighting any battles with words."

"I give you my word, Des. I will confine my writing to my journal and my speaking to the local church when I get to preach sermons. OK"?

She wrapped her arms around me. "I love you so much Darlene. You have given up so much to make me part of your life and I know that God has a ministry for us that will continue to touch lives."

"I believe that also Des. I want to protect our privacy and just grow old together"! I chuckled. "Well, the growing old part is something I don't want to really think about. I wish I'd met you years ago. You could have saved me from all those years of struggling with my sexual orientation."

"We have today…and for as many years that God gives us together. I just don't want to give my parents any reason to cut off our relationship at this point in my life. They have spent their entire life in the Baptist Church, and hearing that homosexuality is an abomination to God. That's not the only issue. I missed out on a lot of years with them because of my marriage to John when he and I ran off together. They stopped going to the Baptist Church because he had been the music director. He left his wife to be with me, and didn't consider how our age difference would impact my parents. He stole my childhood, and I didn't realize it at the time. I feel like I need to get to know my parents again. I want for them to know and love you too, Darlene," she paused. "You saved my life by bringing me to your home and loving me so unconditionally. Our relationship shouldn't matter, but it will to them. I don't think I would have…"

"Hey, none of that! God knew the timing and He alone knows when we will be called home. He is the one that brought us together, and we can celebrate that." I hesitated. "Hey, speaking of your folks, why don't we invite them up for the holidays so they can get to know me a bit better?"

She looked around the house. "We can do that. Let's just make sure any pictures of us being affectionate are put away for their visit"!

I laughed. "Ok, we'll de-dyke the house and put away any of my books that might pop up when they are looking at the book shelves!"

On that first holiday together, and for the many that followed, we made sure that there was nothing to draw attention to the fact we were any more than roommates. Des had her bedroom, which she graciously gave up for her folks, and spent the night in my room. Her parents never asked, and we never offered any information other than that we were best friends, and we cared for one another.

We shared with them our vacation photos (minus any that might cause questions), and her family became accustomed to the fact that we were together on every trip or holiday. I encouraged Des to spend time with her parents and work on healing the wounds of her childhood. Many memories plagued her dreams. It was a constant effort to feel acceptance from her parents without trying to be being 'perfect'. Our relationship as a gay couple would have driven the wedge further between them. Des was never comfortable with the option of sharing our commitment with them. We were talking one day and she made a statement that would prove prophetic.

"I have decided that if I die before you, that you can tell my parents and my brother all about us…It won't matter to me then." She smiled that broad beautiful smile that always seemed to be a bit mischievous. "But that's the only time you can tell them."

"Right" I scoffed. "And what if I die before you"?

"Then I won't have to tell them, will I"? She gazed at me intently. "You better not die. You promised you would never leave me, and you know I couldn't handle being without you"!

"Well then, let's agree to neither one of us die until we're very, very old." I put my arms around her. "Des, I don't know how I lived before God brought us together, and I don't think I could keep on living if anything ever happened to you."

We lived as if we had forever, and we had a lot of years to grow more deeply in love. God was using our lives to reach out to others, and together we were an unbeatable team.

Chapter Three
GOD'S GIFTS AND CALLING ARE WITHOUT REPENTANCE

In so many ways, my life was different. I no longer spent my vacation days traveling across the country on speaking engagements. I didn't have to get up each Sunday morning to attend church or teach a Bible class. I didn't feel the stress of being on a spiritual pedestal, or having to be the poster child of ex-gay ministry.

I was happy to be in a church where I could be involved in ministry, but not have to be the leader. Our lives were focused on God, and also learning how to love one another and be present in our relationship.

It would have been easy to be resentful and angry at how our Christian friends had exposed and betrayed our confidence. I thought more than once how nice it would be to never become involved in any type of ministry. Then I would remember the verse in Romans 11: 29 "For the gifts and calling of God are without repentance." KJV.

God's call on my life was a spiritual teacher and minister. I had no doubt that He had gifted me to communicate His principles to others. That call on my heart had taken a different focus, and for this time in my life, it seemed that I was to be content to teach Bible studies and spend time reading the Bible with Des. We talked for hours about God's intent for us as gay and lesbian children.

The more I read the Bible, and not just selected verses, the more convinced I was that God not only loved us, but had brought us together to share our lives as a couple. Although Des was not comfortable sharing her orientation with her family, she was committed to living the rest of our lives together.

We continued to fellowship at the Lutheran church for almost two years. Then, a split occurred in the church over a moral issue regarding the pastor. Our lives were shattered as we had developed a strong relationship with him and his family. There were months of court appearances and testimony against our friend. The majority of church members sided against the pastor and he was removed from leadership. Des and I chose to remain friends and stand with him and his family during the process. We were in the position of choosing sides, and we knew that our church home as we had known it, was destroyed. Howard was convicted of the charges and sentenced to prison. His family life was destroyed, but our friendship continued as did our support for him personally. We opted to leave the church and start once more to find our place in the Christian world where we could be accepted as a couple.

We spent months visiting gay churches, straight churches, as well as open and affirming churches. The things we liked about each one still left us feeling empty. We enjoyed the worship at larger congregations, but we were not happy when the sermons addressed homosexuality as a sin. We couldn't worship in the freedom of being a gay couple. The Gay churches we visited were small congregations and often spent the Bible teaching time on verses that were used by the religious right to condemn and clobber the gay community.

My heart longed to find that place where spiritual and social needs could both be satisfied. Des and I were both discouraged with the search.

I continued to receive letters and phone calls from men and women who were struggling with homosexual feelings and felt condemned by the church. I purposed to share God's love with each contact, and although I couldn't point them to a church who would accept them, I could tell them about a loving God who did accept them. I knew only that God had brought me on this journey, and wanted me to tell my story with those who contacted me.

On several occasions, I would receive calls from other Exodus leaders. At first, the conversations were of concern for how I was doing since I had left ministry. Then, I would hear of their struggles and how they feared being exposed. One married woman was again struggling with her lesbianism, and was involved with another woman in her support group. I assured her that I would not break confidence and that she could call me anytime. One call was from a single female leader who had been moved into leadership within her support group. She was struggling with attraction to a woman in her group and was fearful of being discovered. She wanted to talk to the leader of the group, but knew that she would be asked to leave, and that thought devastated

her. I promised to pray and encouraged her to call me anytime. One
male leader called when he became involved with another man in his
support group. He was overwhelmed with guilt because he thought
he was healed. I also promised him I would be available to talk and
pray anytime and would not betray their confidences. I kept my word
to them, but spent hours talking to God about the anger I felt. Why
were there so many people who felt they had the definitive last word
on what God thought about our sexuality? Were the years I spent in
Exodus talking about freedom really so shrouded in fear? What would
happen if everyone just spoke honestly and openly about their feelings?
These were a few of the questions that haunted me. But there were
more serious questions that crept into my thoughts.

How much harm had I done to others through the years when I told
them they could change their orientation? What about all the parents
I had encouraged to use tough love with their kids, and accept them,
but not the "sinful" behavior of their loved ones. How many people had
been left in despair when they did all the things I encouraged them
to do, and the feelings never changed? How could I ever help anyone
to receive God's love if it was always conditional? I had wanted to help
others, but I secretly wondered if I had ever helped anyone.

Des assured me that I had helped her to draw closer to the Lord,
and that our love had caused her to accept God's love more fully. That
convinced me that any sermon I preached or article I wrote in the
future needed to proclaim God's unconditional love and acceptance
for everyone, exactly as He had created them. That meant that Gay and
Lesbian people needed to know God's love just as heterosexual people
needed to know God loved and accepted them. I prayed for the right
place for us to worship with others of like mind and spirit.

Within a matter of weeks my prayer was answered. Des and I had
attended a Pride Celebration in Oakland. There were booths with food,
trinkets, and some with information on Gay and Lesbian churches
in the San Francisco/East Bay area. We stopped at one booth and
picked up a flyer. It was the Faith Full Gospel Fellowship meeting in
San Leandro. There appeared to be a good mix of men and women,
and after some discussion with them, we agreed to give them a try the
following Sunday.

It was with some apprehension that we walked into the church
service the next Sunday evening. We liked the fact that services were
in the evening, so that we could still be free to visit other churches in
the morning, or just go to the beach. A lot of our time was spent at the
ocean, just talking together and often reading the Bible and sharing
communion elements. God had drawn our hearts together spiritually
and continued to minister to our wounded spirits.

It was a risk to seek out other Gay Christians, although we longed for fellowship with other women and men who were committed to Jesus Christ. We wanted other couples to share our life and our home, not just accept us as a couple. This was the prayer we had as we entered Faith Full Gospel that first night.

The service style was one of praise and a lot of hand clapping. I felt at home. Des was more cautious. The pastor was a former Pentecostal minister who had been kicked out of his church because of his homosexual orientation. He had two children from his former marriage, and was currently not partnered with anyone. The senior elder was a woman in her 40's who was dating a woman she had met on the internet. Both of them appeared to have a strong commitment to Christ and were very friendly. Cherie and Sandy were the first to welcome us to the service. They had been at the booth the day we stopped during the Oakland Pride celebration. One by one, the members of the church came over and introduced themselves and welcomed us to their fellowship.

The pastor's sermon was Bible based and not geared at attacking the mainline Christian right. He spoke for about a half hour, closed with prayer and everyone was dismissed to a fellowship hall for coffee and dessert. This, we learned, was the time allowed for extended fellowship.

Without hesitation, I shared my personal journey with the Foursquare Church, as well as my involvement with Exodus International. We shared how we had been brought together at a women's conference and knew immediately that it was God's plan for us to share our lives together.

Des shared with them the hurt and rejection she experienced with the betrayal of confidence from our group in exposing us to Exodus and my church leadership. We believed in the outreach to people who struggled with their homosexual orientation, and had wanted the group to continue. We explained how that option was severed when the small group leaders felt we needed to be disciplined and we were forced to confront our group and terminate the ministry. I had resigned from Exodus leadership, and then my senior pastor asked me to leave the church and all ministries. I had complied, knowing that my life was committed to God, and to Des and that He would open new doors of ministry. We were open to this church being the place for a fresh start.

The pastor, whom I will call Alan, listened with interest. "I'm sure you will find this a place to rest and fellowship, and when you are ready to be more involved in the life of the church, there will be a place for you." He spoke from the position of one who had also been deeply wounded by the Christian Church, and shared that he never wanted for anyone to feel less that totally accepted by Jesus Christ. He also shared that he knew it would take time to heal emotionally and spiritually, and they would do anything they could to help us on that journey!

We left that night with new encouragement, and a desire to open our hearts to this group of Gay Christian brothers and sisters. God was once again confirming His presence in a community that has experienced such deep rejection from those who name the name of Christ, but do not accept homosexuals.

Des was quiet on the way home.

"What's going on honey"? I asked. "Didn't you feel comfortable there"?

"Yes," She paused. "I just don't want to get involved in the politics of church organization and have you making our lives more public as a spokesperson for Gay rights. You've spent all those years as an ex-gay spokesperson, and we see how that ended up. I don't want you on television and in the pulpit for Gay rights. I just want us to live a quiet life, have friends who are gay and grow in our faith."

"I hear what you are saying, Des. I have no intention of getting on someone's band wagon and attacking those who think they speak for God in condemning homosexuals."

She reached over and took my hand. "Promise me that we won't get caught up in that agenda."

I squeezed her hand. "I promise, honey. I won't go public with our lives or fight for any rights until you give the word." I chuckled. "But, can I teach Sunday school sometime"?

"You can teach in the local church any time you have the opportunity. I just don't want us to be front page news. You know I don't want to hurt my family, and I know what their reaction would be if they knew about us."

"I won't do anything to put you in that position, Des. All they ever need to know is that I love you with all my heart and you are my very best friend."

She leaned over and kissed me on the cheek. "You're my very best friend too, Darlene. I know that God is leading our lives and that He will show us what to do either at this church or someplace else."

In the following weeks, we attended services and asked a lot of questions about the church beliefs and structure. We began attending classes to pursue membership affiliation and attended their annual planning meeting. The pastor asked me to speak on an upcoming Sunday service, and I accepted. Des joined with a few of the singers to form a worship team for the service. She agreed to sing a solo the night that I would be speaking. We were settling in to a routine and once again God was opening doors of ministry.

Cherie and Sandy were becoming friends outside of the Sunday worship times. We joined with them for mid- week Bible studies and at least once a week we would go out to dinner. We met other Christian lesbians through our relationship with Sandy and Cherie, and both Des and I were feeling more settled in our faith and our relationship.

I still received calls from readers of my books and articles. I became bolder in sharing my current relationship and encouraged them to seek a deeper relationship with Jesus and He would lead them on their path. I shared that my journey was for a committed relationship, but only God could say if that was their journey.

I explained that while I was in a committed relationship with Des, I had great peace that I was living out my faith and that God was directing our lives. I thought often about my last conversation with my editor, Jane. It brought me great sorrow to know that she could no longer be my friend based solely upon our common faith in Jesus Christ. When our conversation had ended, I told her that I hoped one day in Heaven that we could be friends. I know that God's grace isn't limited to our understanding of human sexuality. I am still saddened that not only our professional relationship, but our personal relationship was no longer acceptable to her.

Once again, Des and I shared many long discussions about our faith. It was evident that we would not be 'accepted' by our mainstream Christian friends, although they profess to still love us. No matter how I studied the Scriptures, I did not find that conditional love was to be the standard we were supposed to embrace. Never once did I read from the pages, "I love you **but…**" God's love is unconditional as is His acceptance. If there are areas to be changed in our lives, (and there still are), then it is the job of the Holy Spirit to convict our hearts and show us the path of change.

Des and I poured over the Scriptures and nowhere could we find the need to change our behavior when it came to loving one another. We dedicated ourselves to live our lives according to our understanding and acceptance of Gods unconditional love for us, and to share that with everyone we met.

It was painful and difficult to let go of long time relationships. Our personal history with so many in the Church had lulled us into feeling that friendships were forever. Des had several close friends that had families the same age as her boys. Several of the women had spent vacations and holidays, and shared meals. They had loved one another as Christian sisters. Almost immediately, she was cut off from contact with the church families, and was isolated from the love of people who had been so much a part of her personal history. It was as if she had not existed in their midst for the past 20 years. Our relationship became the topic of mid-week prayer meetings.

I was crushed emotionally as I watched her struggle with the loss of her past. I had expected that Exodus and my Christian network would abandon me. But I was unprepared for the emotional devastation that Des was experiencing. I was feeling very guilty. If we had not fallen in love, she would still be acceptable to her family and friends. The reality was that she would probably not be alive if she had stayed with John. She felt she was a failure as a mother, and still felt rejection from her own mother.

On more that one occasion, we held each other and wept. There was no way to make others accept and love us when they felt we were living in "sin". There was no way to walk through the Scriptures with them and have the Spirit open their hearts to unconditional love and acceptance for all people.

I was reminded often of the saying, "Don't confuse me with facts, my mind is made up!"

We began to pray for our family and Christian friends in specific terms. It was up to God to turn their hearts, and if He didn't, then we would continue to love and accept them, but we would not have the same expectation. Our lives were committed to one another and God was the keeper of our hearts. We were open to new friendships within the Gay community, but even there we were hesitant to embrace an unconditional acceptance.

Our friendship with Cherie and Sandy was the closest relationship we had with anyone in the gay community. They had been together for some time and wanted to have a commitment ceremony to declare their love for one another. They asked me if I would perform their ceremony. I was honored to accept, and on the appointed day in September, a small group went to Napa for a Hot Air Balloon ride and a wedding ceremony. Through our friendship with Sandy and Cherie, we had met Becky, a single lesbian. Des and Becky were the witnesses. (Actually, they were the only ones who would go up in the hot air balloon). We were with a group of straight folks who enjoyed the wedding and ceremony that we performed high above the vineyards of Napa Valley. I was thrilled to be affirmed as a pastor called by God to serve those in the Gay community.

Other weddings and a few funerals followed those days of reclaiming my spiritual calling. Life with Des as my spiritual partner and lover had God's approval. We were looking forward to growing old together. It no longer mattered what the past ministry had been, we knew God had something special planned for our lives.

The holidays were over and family commitments had been kept. We were making plans to go someplace special to celebrate Des' birthday in January. Without warning, she received the phone call that changed both our lives forever.

Chapter Four
Breast Cancer Opens New Doors

I was at work, sitting at my desk when the phone rang. I reached over and picked up the receiver. "Underwriting, this is Darlene." I clicked on the computer, expecting it to be a client.

"It's just me, honey." Des' voice was shaky.

"Hi. What's going on"? I leaned back in my chair and waited.

"I just got a call from Kaiser. They want me to come back in today for a retake on my mammogram." She paused. "They said there is something suspicious on the film." She began to cry. "I'm really scared."

My voice softened. "It's probably nothing honey. Don't worry. What time do you have to be there? I'll meet you at the hospital." I began to shut down my computer and clear my calendar for the rest of the day.

"They have a spot open at three. The doctor said she wants to talk to me after the new films are taken." Her voice was just a whisper. "Darlene, what if it's cancer"?

"Whatever it is, we'll handle it together." I felt like someone had just kicked me in the stomach at the thought of this spot being cancer. Des would be turning 42 in just a few days and this wasn't the present I was planning on giving her. I glanced at the clock. I'll leave work now and meet you in the parking lot." I hung up the phone as a growing lump in my throat erupted into tears down my cheeks. I quickly wiped them away and grabbed my keys as I dialed my boss's extension.

"I have a family emergency", I blurted. "I need to leave for the rest of the day."

"That's fine. Let your team know that you're leaving. You can make up the time."

"Thanks," I murmured. I walked calmly through the department, my mind racing with all the fears hidden in that one word…Cancer.

I drove to the hospital and Des was already in the parking lot. I parked beside her and could tell immediately that she had been crying. I walked to her green Ford van and opened the door. Without a word, I wrapped my arms around her shoulders and held her close. "It will be all right honey…no matter what, we have the Lord, and He is still in charge of our lives.

I wiped the moisture from her cheeks. "I love you, Des. We will face this together."

"I know", she whispered. "Maybe it's nothing. I'm just so scared of cancer and we know so many people who have breast cancer. I just wasn't expecting a call like this."

"Well, let's go get the new mammogram and talk with the doctor." I took her hand and we walked into the hospital. Twenty minutes later we were sitting in the doctor's office hearing words that seemed foreign to us.

"This mammogram is just to confirm what I already saw on your films. You have a cancerous lump in your left breast, about the two o'clock position. I want to schedule you for a biopsy to see if there are clear margins and to test for lymph node involvement." She paused. "You can go down to surgery when you leave here and schedule for those procedures." She was matter of fact in her tone.

"Could there be some mistake"? I interjected. "I mean, could it just be a benign lump or something other than cancer"?

"No," she responded. "The cells have a unique shape. We know its cancer. The surgeon will discuss treatments with you after the biopsy."

I held Des' hand in a vice grip. "It's ok, honey. We can't let fear control our thinking. We'll take this one step at a time." I stood and pulled Des up next to me. "Thank you, doctor. We'll deal with whatever the future holds."

The doctor stood and extended her hand. "I'm sorry."

The next few hours were filled with making appointments and deciding who we wanted to tell. "Let's just go home and let this all absorb in our minds." I suggested. "I don't think I can handle talking with anyone right now."

I followed her home and we walked inside. We were exhausted and went into the bedroom and lay on the bed for hours, just holding each other and crying what would be the first of many tears. "_Why, God, Why_" **???** my brain was spinning. I knew I was asking the universal question with no answer. We had dozens of questions that needed answers in regards to how we would handle this cancer and how it would affect our lives. One thing that we were agreed upon from the very start was that it wasn't Des who had cancer, **we** had cancer and **we** would fight it together! That first night we didn't call anyone with the news, we just talked and prayed and cried.

With the morning came time to make several decisions. Des was self employed in a mobile uniform business. She had medical clients all over the bay area. Her project for the day was to make calls and let the doctor's offices and nurses know that her schedule would be changed in the next couple of weeks. We had a couple of days before the biopsy and couldn't make any long term decisions until we found out those results.

I took the day off work so that we could begin to organize our life. Des' relationship with her parents had begun to heal since she had moved with me to Hayward. They had just spent Christmas with us. Des had spent many hours talking about the pain of her childhood and why she had made the decision to marry a man 25 years older. That marriage had been the source of much strife between them, and her parents were not ready to forget all the pain it had caused. Des told them that the only good thing that had come from the marriage was her two sons. Today, it only seemed important to let her parents know about the breast cancer. Their past differences would have to heal over time.

I sat beside her on the couch as she dialed her parent's number in southern California. She put the phone on speaker, so I could hear the conversation. Her father answered the phone. "Hello" he said from the speaker.

"Hi Daddy, it's me, Des." She took a deep breath, and I saw tears begin to trickle down her cheeks.

"Hi honey. How are you today"? His voice was friendly.

"I have some bad news, Daddy. I have breast cancer." She waited for a response.

"Oh no," He said with a shocked tone. "When? How did they find it? What are they going to do"? His questions rambled on, and many had no answers at that point. "Do you need for us to come back up there? Do you need money for anything"?

"No Daddy. I just wanted to let you and Mother know. I will have a biopsy this week and then they will tell me what will happen. I'm still in shock." The tears were flowing and her voice was choked with emotion. "I'll let you know more when I find out." She hung the phone back on the receiver, and once more we held each other and wept.

Des made several calls that morning. She contacted each of her sons, as well as her former husband. I watched her face as she finished talking with John.

"You know honey; there is something else that needs to be done as soon as possible." I paused, not wanting to add additional stress at this time. "We need to contact an attorney and get your divorce finalized. We don't know what the future holds, but I don't want there to be any question as to legal matters as far as our relationship is concerned."

She nodded. "Will you find someone and make us an appointment"?

"I'll take care of that today. We need to get our wills taken care of at the same time, and make sure that you have no legal obligations connected with that marriage." I paused. "We will make provisions for the boys as long as they are minors. John might have physical custody, but you need to have your legal rights protected for joint custody. They might not want anything to do with you right now, but that can change in the future."

The rest of that day was filled with phone calls to attorneys, to the American Cancer society for information, and to dozens of Des' clients.

Although the majority of my Christian friends had long since abandoned our friendship, there were a few special people that I needed to contact.

The first was Marie Hollowell. She was the former dean of woman from my college days and the woman I called Mom. Marie had told me many years ago at the time of my first lesbian experience, that she would only reject me when Jesus did. So many college friends had walked out of my life when Linda and I became involved in a relationship during my freshman year. Marie's steadfast love during that emotional time, and through all the years that followed, was something I had grown to count on through every relationship. She was always an encouragement and prayerful support as I tried to reconcile Christianity and homosexuality. I had called her when Des and I got together and told her how I felt God had brought us together as a Christian couple. Although she wasn't convinced that a sexual relationship was Biblical, she was convinced that God and I were irrevocably connected and she would do no less than love and pray for us to live our lives for Him. She was now over 70 years of age and had also experienced a breast cancer diagnosis several years earlier. I picked up the phone to call and ask for prayers.

Marie lived in Seattle and no longer traveled much, but assured me that she would come for a visit as soon as we got our surgery schedule and would help in any way she could. We put her on the schedule for a few weeks down the line.

My next call was to a Christian writer friend that I'd known over ten years. Bonnie and I had met at Mt. Hermon just after I had 'become straight' and she had been one of the first to read the manuscript for my first book. She and her husband had accepted me as a member of the family. Her knowledge of homosexuality was pretty much limited to the story of my life and my work with Exodus ministry. She had believed my life was 'delivered' from homosexuality, because my writings had detailed out the path of freedom.

When Des and I found one another, and my journey changed, I had gone to see Bonnie and Dennis to tell them, before they heard it through the prayer requests for fallen church leaders! Our conversation had been intense.

Bonnie sat in her blue flowered rocker. She listened to my account of how Des and I had met, and how for the first time I felt like a puzzle piece had snapped into place, completing the picture. I told her how I felt completed and whole, instead of isolated and empty and no longer had to keep busy in order to find meaning in serving Christ.

She looked thoughtful. "Here's what I don't understand, Darlene. I know you. I love you and I know that you have a personal relationship with the Lord. Your book tells in detail how you always felt that your lesbianism was a demonic possession and you were delivered from those demons through prayer. Does this mean that you are demon possessed again?"

I chuckled aloud. "No, that's not what it means." I sighed. "When I wrote both of my books back in the late 80's, I thought I had all the answers. I had a lot of people praying for me. I really felt that since I was not experiencing attraction for women, that I was delivered from homosexuality. I also used to think that women who became lesbians had all experienced sexual abuse. I took my own experience and applied it to all situations, because many of the women I counseled had been victims of sexual and physical abuse as children." I paused, and then continued. "Here is what I have learned since the final chapters of Long Road to Love and Strangers in a Christian Land were written. Many women are victims of abuse, and never become lesbians. Many women and men are raped and never become homosexual. What does happen is that there are broken places in the spirit that only God can heal. I have been in many hours of psychotherapy and prayer healing in the past years since those books. I'm sure that Christians cannot be demon possessed, but there can and are areas of demonic oppression. Those wounds and bondages are broken by the power of God's love and Jesus precious blood. I have been delivered, not from the bondage of lesbianism, but the bondage to a wounded spirit that was so afraid of the masculine that had abused me. I am free to be the woman God created me to be, and to experience physical and emotional love with women, not out of fear, but out of freedom. My sexual orientation toward women is a gift from God, just as my twin sisters' sexual orientation toward men is her natural gift from God." I looked at Bonnie. "Does this make sense to you"?

"Yes, it makes sense." She hesitated. "I just thought you had all the answers when you wrote your book because it made sense to my theology. I think what the church wants to hear is that homosexuality is a choice, and you all can change if you kick the devil out of your life"!

I laughed. "That would be simple. Do you think it would work with fat cells and all of the other things we want to change in our lives? Seriously, if my homosexual orientation were a choice, then it could be classified as a sin. There is no place in Scripture where Jesus says one word about the sin of homosexuality. Gluttony however is another matter." I chuckled. "I recently heard there are only eight scriptures directed at the homosexual and over three hundred addressing heterosexual behavior. I guess God knew who needed the most supervision! The Bible addresses many topics and states that of faith, hope and love, the greatest of these, is love."

The tension between us was eased. Bonnie spoke quietly. "Your position on being Christian and Gay are not going to be any more popular with the church than being ex-gay was with the homosexual community. I believe you are being guided by the Lord, and I will never love you any less for your life with Des. I love her for loving you, and I'm sure that we will have it all figured out by the time we get to heaven."

"I hope it doesn't take that long," I had ended our talk with a confirmed feeling of acceptance.

Today, I made the call to share with her about Des' breast cancer. She offered prayers and a visit soon, with a warm meal.

I had a couple more calls to make. I was feeling more reaffirmed that not all of God's kids had cut off contact due to Des and my commitment to one another.

My next call was to my friend Dianne. Our history also dated back over ten years. Dianne was five years older than I, and we shared the same birth month. We had met at the Assembly of God Church and became involved in the singles ministry. When I told her about my past involvement in the gay community she thought for a moment then responded, "I don't think your background history is any worse than mine. I was a hippy in the 60's and lived in Berkeley. God is only concerned about how we are responding to His voice and His love in the now. I'm not shocked by any of your stories, I see only the woman you are right now." Thus began a friendship that included vacation trips, attending Bible school and co- teaching Sunday school classes. Dianne had gone on to earn her degree at Fuller Theological Seminary, and was gifted in the area of counseling.

She had become one of my most ardent supporters when I had started the ex-gay ministry. When I met Des and knew that my life was about to change in many ways, Dianne was one of the first people I called. I was apprehensive about her response.

"Hi, Dianne, do you have a few minutes to talk"? I was forming my words in my brain as I waited.

"Oh! Hi Darlene. What's happening"?

"Well, I wanted to tell you the news." I hesitated, and then blurted the string of events. "I've been kicked out of Exodus ministry, my church has asked me to leave, my books are being pulled from circulation, and I've fallen in love with the most wonderful Christian woman in the world!"

"Wow," she exhaled with a deep sigh. "I think you better start with the last statement. I suspect that everything else is a result of this woman." She paused, "When did this all happen"?

"It's been in the last month or so." I began to tell the story of how Des and I had met at the woman's retreat where I was speaking. I shared how we both knew immediately that God was bringing us together. "Dianne, it's like all the counseling and healing that God has been working in my heart for the past several years wasn't to make me straight, but to prepare me for this relationship with Des. I feel so complete and I have no doubts at all that God has brought us together."

"I can see why the other events have happened. Did you go to your pastor and the Exodus board"?

"No on both accounts." I hesitated, and then continued. "The members of the group felt like it was their responsibility to tell Exodus I was involved in a "sinful" relationship. I had wanted to turn the ministry over to the leaders, and just leave quietly. Mark felt that exposure would bring me to my senses and cause me to "repent". Here's the thing Dianne. For the first time in my life, I don't feel like I've anything to repent of, and my relationship with Des is not sin."

"First of all, our friendship doesn't depend on your being gay." She paused. "How does your new theology fit with everything you've been teaching for the past ten years"?

"That's the strange thing, Dianne. In Romans Chapter one, the Bible talks about women leaving the natural relations for unnatural ones. We've always picked one or two verses from this section to show how homosexuality is the sin of all sins. I heard it from the pulpit and from all the Exodus teaching, but when I went back and took the full context of Chapter One and Two of Romans, the message is quite different! I don't hate God or refuse to hear His words, and I'm not full of envy, murder and all the rest of the things on the list."

"I can affirm that, based upon our conversations," she interjected.

I took a deep breath and then continued. "The teachings are wrong. They are taking a partial truth and applying it to a sexual orientation that is a gift of God the same as a heterosexual orientation. This chapter is about behavior toward one another and a hostile attitude toward the things of God; it has nothing to do with calling homosexuality sin." I was on a roll and continued to expound my revelations. "The Scripture says in I Corinthians 6:9-11 that wicked people, sexually immoral, idolaters, adulterers, thieves, greedy, drunkards, and homosexual offenders, among a lot of other folks will not inherit the kingdom of God. This section of scripture is one of the main pieces used to condemn homosexuality. Once again, when you go back and read the entire section, it doesn't say what we have reported it to say in condemnation of homosexuality.'

Dianne spoke softly. "Most of what Paul had to say was dealing with chastity and a Christian life that reflected the life of Christ. I don't think he was trying to categorize all the sins that men could commit."

"I agree. Paul even states later that everything is permissible for him but not everything is beneficial." I hardly took a breath. "This is what I've discovered in the past couple of months. Not only is it important to look at the culture of the day in which the Scripture was written, but we need to look at the culture of the day in which Scripture was revised! The word homosexual has not always been part of the text, and we just assume that it has always been there. What I have been teaching, and what Exodus as a whole is teaching is only part of the truth. God does want us to live in a way that brings glory to Him and causes us to be whole, not fragmented persons. This is the exciting thing for me. The more whole I am becoming, the more I realize God intends for me to embrace the woman He created. That woman is free to love another woman, and not have to feel that I need a man to complete me! This is the natural direction for my sexuality, because God gave me the gift of homosexuality. I've been trying to give it back and take on a role that would make me acceptable to the church. I finally heard His voice telling me that Des was the woman He had prepared me to receive and that we should grow together as a Christian couple, and embrace love as His true gift."

There was silence on the other end of the line for just a moment. "Are you through?" She asked quietly.

"I am at least for the moment." I replied.

"Well, here is what I think. You know that I've looked long and hard at the Scriptures. The Hebrew language has many meanings for one word, and we have translated many words with just one meaning. The Greek is more specific in its language; however I'm not convinced that we should be taking every verse literally. I think as long as your heart does not condemn you, it certainly isn't my place to do that. The Holy Spirit leads us into all truth, and I think that you are moving in the right direction by searching the Scripture. I'm sorry that you are out of ministry because I believe that God's calling on your life is as a spiritual teacher. I suppose this makes you my gay Christian sister. I will continue to support you in any way God leads."

"Really"? I was shocked at such openness.

"Yes, and now my only question is when do I get to meet Des"?

That conversation had opened the door for many hours of conversation with the three of us, and a fresh look at what the Hebrew and Greek Texts meant when they spoke of relationships between all individuals. I was really proud to have a friend who could use her Theology degree to find a basis for inclusion instead of exclusion.

On this day, my call was for emotional and prayer support. Des had breast cancer and the days ahead seemed cloudy at best. I dialed Dianne's number at work.

"Hello. This is Dianne", the familiar voice brought comfort.

"Dianne, its Darlene. I won't keep you long. Des just found out she has breast cancer. We're having a biopsy in two days to determine what action will be taken. Will you please pray?"

"I'm so sorry, Darlene. I will come be with you at the hospital. Tell me when and where."

I gave her the details then hung up. Des was sitting on the couch watching me.

"We've been so focused for months on all the people who rejected us that I had forgotten about all the people who love and accept us as a couple." The tears were once again streaming down her cheeks.

"I know honey, it's amazing to me." I walked over and sat beside her. "We're going to make it through this thing. I know that God didn't bring us together to let cancer take you away." I wrapped my arms around her and held her to my chest. "I love you so much, Des and there's nothing I won't do to fight this disease. We will do whatever it takes."

The next few days were filled with more calls to friends and family. I made an appointment with an attorney to begin the paperwork to complete Des' divorce. We established new wills, to protect her assets and mine, and make provision for her sons in the event of her death while they were still minors. I felt useful while I was doing tasks that would prepare us for the future. In the silent times, I felt so helpless over this little word that now hung over our lives like a giant hammer, ready to smash our hearts and our future into a million pieces.

On the night before Des' biopsy we were sitting on the couch and I picked up the Bible. I opened up to Psalm 139 and began to read aloud.

"For you created my inmost being; you knit me together in my mother's womb. I praise you because I am fearfully and wonderfully made; your works are wonderful. I know that full well. My frame was not hidden from you when I was made in the secret place. When I was woven together in the depths of the earth, your eyes saw my unformed body. All the days ordained for me were written in your book before one of them came to be. How precious to me are your thoughts O God, how vast is the sum of them." Ps 139:13-17. NIV.

I reached over and took her hand. "Nothing that happens to us surprises God. He has just let us in on the information." I blinked back my tears and tried to swallow the lump in my throat. "The only guarantee we have as Christians is that Jesus will never leave or forsake us Des. We can trust Him to be with us through this procedure and the days ahead."

"I know" she whispered. "I'll just be glad when we know how bad it is and what they are going to do."

"We'll know soon enough. The next few weeks are going to be rough. I want for us to go to Big Sur this weekend and just spend time at the ocean. We need to make plans, and you will need to rest after the biopsy. It will probably take awhile for the results."

Her body melted against me and she whispered, more to God than to me. "I'm so scared."

"I know honey, I am scared too. God has promised us the strength we need, and a lot of people are praying." We sat for a long time then went to bed.

The next morning I took Des to the hospital. Several friends from church were in the lobby, and Dianne was just walking in from the parking lot. After hugs and introductions all of us walked to the surgery waiting room. The surgeon came out to talk with us prior to the procedure. "Are you all family"? He looked at the group.

"We're part of God's family, and these are our prayer support." I grinned.

"That's a good thing. I'm a Christian too, so we're all in good hands." He looked at Des. "Are you ready for this"?

"I'm anxious to get it done." She responded. "Will I be awake for the whole thing"?

"Yes," he replied. "We'll remove the lump and send it to pathology while you're still on the table. They will let us know how extensive it is, and the course of treatment."

"We'll know that today"? I questioned.

"Yes. I want to be aggressive in our treatment. If we get clear margins and there is no lymph node involvement, then just removing the lump might be all we need to do."

I put my arms around Des and kissed her lightly on the cheek. "We'll be right here praying." My heart felt like it was breaking. "I'd go in with you if I could"

The doctor spoke up. "The operation room has to be sanitary. I'll take good care of her." She followed him into the surgery lab.

It was an hour later when Dr. Ku emerged from the room. "She's still under some mild sedation, so it will be a few more minutes before she can leave. You can come help her dress, if you'd like."

"Sure," I looked at him questioningly. "Do you have the results from the lab"?

"Yes," he said quietly. "There's good news and bad. The good news is no lymph nodes are apparently involved, the bad is that we were unable to get clear margins on the tumor."

"So that means…" my sentence faded away.

"We will be scheduling her for a mastectomy next week." You'll be talking with the oncologist as to the chemotherapy regiment that he will prescribe. That will happen a few weeks after surgery.

"Does she know"? I asked as we walked toward the room. My head was spinning.

"Yes, I told her." He held the door.

Des was lying under a sheet. She reached out for me and squeezed my hand. The look on her face was one of shock.

"Let's get you dressed and out of here." I helped her sit up and pulled her sweatshirt over her head. "You don't need the rest of it, I'm sure you're going to be sore when this pain killer wears off." I helped her off the table and put my arm around her as we walked toward the waiting room.

"Will you tell them"? She whispered.

"Yes," I replied. "Then we'll get you home to rest, and I'll come back and take care of the arrangements for surgery next week."

"We've got to call Daddy and Mother." The tears welled up in her eyes.

"We'll do it at home, honey. Just hold on to me."

Once in the waiting room, I quickly shared the news with everyone and asked for their continued prayers. Someone brought a wheelchair, and we headed toward the parking lot.

"Please tell everyone at church, and keep us on the prayer list." I looked at Dianne. "Do you want to come to the house for awhile"?

"Sure. I'll do what I can to help you get Des settled. I know you have things to handle before her surgery."

Dianne followed us home and agreed to stay with Des while I ran errands. I went to the hospital and got the list of instructions for the day of surgery. On the way back home I stopped by my office and scheduled several days of vacation so that I could care for Des after her surgery. I contacted the divorce attorney and arranged for the information to be handled by telephone, until Des would need to sign the papers. I would deliver them in person to John, to avoid processing fees.

While I was gone, Des had called her parents and they would be coming back to Hayward for her surgery. This time, they decided to stay in a motel close by, rather than at our home. I was relieved to have that stress removed, since I didn't know what we were facing after the surgery and her release from the hospital.

Dianne stayed for several hours. She promised to return on the day of surgery and would be praying for us in the days ahead. I was thankful for the special friendship that we shared. I learned that day, that a true friend is one you can sit silently with in the same room and not feel compelled to explain your feelings, or even talk. The comfort shared is in the act of just being present.

The rest of the evening was filled with phone calls from friends and Des' clients calling to find out her diagnosis from the biopsy. So many were Christians, and assured us that they would not only be praying, but put her name on their church prayer lists.

My sisters called from Washington and offered their words of concern and love. The thing that was so amazing is that Des wanted to talk with each caller. She shared her faith in God and confidence that no matter what the outcome, she knew God was in control. As I listened to the conversations, I realized that Cancer had opened a new door of ministry.

I was glad we had plans for the weekend to Celebrate Des' Birthday. She was going to be 42 this year and I had planned the special trip to Big Sur and the ocean. The phone calls were beginning to be annoying, and we both needed some quiet time.

The setting was perfect. We had a cabin with a fireplace set along the edge of a meadow. The ocean was within a half mile, and we could drive to the beach just to watch the waves.

We talked of all the plans we'd made in the past three years and how quickly life's focus had changed. We wanted to grow old together and travel the United States when we retired. Now, the only plan we had was to make it through each day and not give in to the fears of having cancer. One thing happened that weekend that created a deep, personal bond between us.

We were lying on the bed in front of the fireplace, watching the flames lick the air. She turned to me and took my hand, placing it on her left breast.

"Will you pray a special commitment prayer for this breast as it leaves my body"? She had tears streaming down her cheeks. "It's been with me all my life and I don't know how to say goodbye."

I pulled her close, keeping my hand gently on the place where the tumor had been. "Lord, I've asked for a lot of things in my life, and now, we're asking that you would help Des be able to say good-by to this breast that has been a part of her for 42 years. It's fed her sons, and brought pleasure to her lovers, and now, it's full of disease. We ask that the surgeons use great skill when removing it next week and that all the cancer would be taken away from the healthy tissue." I paused. "Lord, we commit this breast into your care, as we commit our lives into your care. Please hold us close in the days ahead."

My tears were streaming down my cheeks, falling as anointing oil upon her bare chest.

Des cupped my face in her hands. "Thank you, Darlene." She paused. "I have one other question for you."

"What's that"? I managed a smile.

"Will you still love me with only one breast and a huge scar"?

"More than ever," I whispered. "More than ever."

Chapter Five
Four Years and Eleven Months

The day of Des' surgery arrived along with two dozen friends, family and well wishers in the waiting room. Her dad and mother were amazed at the support from our church friends, and some obviously gay couples. I watched them carefully, but today was not the time for explanations of our friends or our relationship. I made sure that her folks had special time with Des before she was wheeled into surgery. I held Des' hand and leaned down to kiss her as I stroked her hair. "I love you Des." I whispered. Then she was wheeled into the surgery room.

It was five hours later when Dr. Ku entered the waiting room. He walked over to me with a smile on his face. "The surgery went fine. She will be in recovery for some time, and then transferred to a room. She will spend one night in the hospital, and then you can take her home." He paused. "I didn't find any evidence of further cancer. The entire tumor was encapsulated and still no evidence of lymph node involvement."

"That's good," I responded. "How long before I can see her"?

He looked at our support group. "Why don't you all go out to lunch, and when you come back I'll see how she's progressing."

Bonnie stood and gave me a hug. "I have to get back to work. I'll check on you tonight."

Dianne joined us. "I need to get back to Santa Cruz, too. I'll be in touch with you this evening." She gave me a big hug. "You'll be fine. Take care of her folks."

Several people from church accompanied her mother and daddy and me as we made our way to the hospital cafeteria. I didn't feel like eating, but since I couldn't get in to see Des, I followed.

An hour and a half passed before I made my way back toward the recovery room. I saw Dr Ku at the end of the hall. "Is she awake yet"? I questioned.

"Yes, they just moved her to room 309." He glanced at the group that was following me. "You need to have no more than two at a time. She probably won't really be awake for several hours."

"I understand." I walked back to the others. "Visitation is limited and she isn't really awake yet. She'll probably be in a lot of pain. I think it's best if her mother and daddy go in for a minute, then we can switch off and you can each just stay for a moment."

I walked up to the 3rd floor with her parents and we walked to Des' room. I stood in the doorway while they went in and stood by the bed. She was still sleeping and was not aware of our presence. I decided other visits would have to wait.

I broke the news to those who were waiting, and extended an invitation to come to the house if they wished to do so. Des' mother and dad came with me and we spent the rest of the day just talking, and making more phone calls. When Harold and Dorothy left for their motel, the house seemed quiet and empty. I felt lost without Des, and although visiting hours were ending at the hospital, I drove there just to be close to her. I walked through the halls and stood outside her room. A nurse passed by.

"Visiting hours are over, but you can see her for a moment. She is still pretty groggy, but she's awake."

I stepped inside and walked to her bed, reaching for her right hand. "Hi honey, it's me." I said quietly.

Her eyes blinked and brought me into focus. A slight smile crept across her lips. "I'm glad you're here. I'm still alive."

"Yes, you are, and will be for a long time!" I looked at tubes and bandages where her left breast had been. "You're the most beautiful woman I know." I whispered as I leaned down and kissed her.

The nurse appeared in the doorway behind me. "She needs her rest. You can come back tomorrow. I think she's only scheduled for an overnight stay."

I leaned down and kissed her forehead. "I'll see you first thing in the morning. Sleep well." I turned and left the room. *God, please keep her in your care. Help her to heal so we can get on with the rest of our lives.* Many prayer thoughts were sent as I drove home to our empty house. This was just the first of many sleepless nights. I sat up for hours writing in my journal and pouring through our photo albums. We had been together almost three years, and it wasn't nearly long enough.

I had read a quote that "Life is what happens while you're making other plans." I knew our life was changing, yet my heart still clung to the plans we had made for travel and for growing old together. I wasn't ready to give up those dreams.

It was about 6:30 am when I decided to call a friend in the mid west. Judy was the Director for an Exodus group ministry. Our friendship had extended beyond the conferences, and when I had been ousted from Exodus, she still maintained contact. Our friendship was strong and she never passed judgments or tried to shame me into leaving Des.

The phone rang twice before she picked up. "Good Morning." She mumbled.

"Hey, this is your California buddy." I paused. "Did I wake you? It's three hours later where you are."

"I was just being lazy today," she responded. "What's happening with you? When are you coming for a visit"?

"It's going to be awhile. Des was diagnosed with breast cancer last week, and had a mastectomy yesterday. She's still in the hospital. I get to bring her home later today.

I don't think we'll be going anywhere for a couple of months."

"I'm really sorry to hear that Darlene. Is there anything I can do"?

"One thing is to please put her on the prayer list at your church. I know that God is with us through this part of the journey too, but it's a side road I didn't know was there." The tightness in my chest and the lump in my throat betrayed my emotional composure. "Judy, I love this woman with all my heart. I don't want to go through life without her."

"What are they saying about her chances of recovery"?

The lump was fairly small, and there was no obvious lymph node involvement. They will put her on six months of chemotherapy once the incision heals. That's all we know right now. It will be six weeks before she can return to her job. She has the mobile uniform shop and has to lift all those bins of heavy uniforms, so that's not going to happen. We might see if we can hire someone to do the lifting for her until her arm muscles are strong again." I paused. "Right now, I just want to get her home so I can take care of her."

"I hear that. I'll put her on the prayer chain and be supportive there. If you need to talk, just give me a call anytime. I mean that, Darlene. There are still a lot of people in Exodus who care about you."

"Sure there are. That's why you are the only one who stays in contact with me." I sighed at the thought. "I guess my idea of friendship is a lot different than having to embrace the same theology as the other person."

"You and I both know that friendship goes deeper than Theology. You were the lesbian they could point to as having changed, and you could speak and write the story. They needed you to be part of the ex-gay story. When that changed for you, they didn't know how to respond.

You are a Christian and love the Lord, but having a same sex lover is not in the Exodus acceptable standards. They need for you to repent so they can restore you to service."

"Well, that's the problem. I have nothing to repent from, and Des is more than a lover. She is my life partner." I hesitated a moment. "So how is it that you and I are still friends"?

She responded quickly. "It's not my place to judge you or to condemn you, or tell you the path that Jesus is leading you. I love you as a friend, and even if we don't have the same view of the Scriptures, our friendship is built on where we do agree. If I saw destructive behavior in your life, I would be the first to confront those issues. All that I know of yours and Des' relationship is healthy and one that seeks to put Christ first. What you do in your bedroom is between you and God. End of story!"

"I guess that's why we're still friends, Judy. Anyway, I just wanted to let you know about Des, and I'll bring you up to date as we find out more details."

"That sounds good Darlene. Hang in there. You'll get through this one day at a time."

"I know, it's just hard to watch Des go through this, and I can't do anything but be with her. "

"That's what she needs. I'll be in touch with you soon." Judy hung up and once again, my house seemed strangely empty.

I decided to shower and get ready for the day. I was just drying myself when the phone rang. I made a dash to pick up the receiver. "Hello"

"Hi honey, it's me. I want you to come to the hospital." Des' voice was weak. "I miss you and didn't sleep very much last night."

"I'll get dressed and be right there. I love you, Des don't forget that."

"I love you too, Darlene." Her voice trailed off in a sleepy tone.

It took me ten minutes to get to the hospital and up on the 3rd. floor. When I walked into her room the nurses were helping her to sit and preparing to change the bandages. I walked to the side where I could see the long line of tubes and a drain ball taped to her abdomen. The scar stretched from the middle of her chest to just under her arm pit, and was stapled together. Des wasn't looking at the wound. She fixed her eyes on me, and I noticed moisture at the edge of her lids.

"I don't want to see it yet," she whispered.

"That's ok, Des. There will be plenty of time." I looked at the nurse. "When I have her home, how do I need to take care of her"?

They went into great detail about keeping the wound clean, and showed me how to empty the drainage ball. There was a list of things to watch out for with the incision. There were three prescriptions that needed to be filled. I took them to the pharmacy so that we would have them with us once they released her.

When I returned to the room, Des' mother and dad were with her. They appeared relieved to see that she was alert. I walked over and gave them hugs. "It's good to see you this morning."

I looked at Des. "I think we get to take our girl home in a couple of hours."

"I'm ready," she murmured. "I have to get a final check from Dr. Ku, and then they can release me."

"I'll take you out for a chocolate milkshake if you want," I offered with a grin.

"All I want is to leave this place and go home to my own bed!" She looked at her parents. "I don't think I'm going to be very good company today. I'm really in a lot of pain."

Her Dad responded. "That's ok, honey. We'll be there if you need anything, but you don't have to entertain us."

We talked for the next hour until the doctor came in on his morning rounds. He examined her incision. "This looks good. She'll be sore for awhile, but it should heal fine. Unless there is an unexpected problem, bring her back in a week and we can talk about the next steps of her recovery." He shook hands with me, and left the room to sign her release.

The week passed quickly for me. I returned to work as her parents were there to tend to meals and any needs that came up in my absence. I would change her bandage every day and empty the drain tube. She still did not want to look at the incision.

By the weekend, she was moving around pretty good, and her folks decided to return to Southern California. I was thrilled to finally be alone with Des and be able to hold her without fear of her parents walking in the room. Our conversation turned often to our future and what plans we could make to get away for a few days.

"Here is the doctor's plan for you." I paused. "In one more week, the staples can be removed. It will be at least a month before you can even consider driving and returning to work. We may have to hire someone to help you lift the uniform bins. In the meantime, it occurred to me that when someone calls needing uniforms, give them our address and I can sell them what they need."

"That's a good idea, Darlene. I can call my regular customers and let them know that the surgery came out fine, and give them the option of coming to me for the next month."

"In the meantime, I need to work during the day, but I can take you for short trips to the beach if you feel up to traveling. We should probably wait on that also, because the seat belt could hurt your chest if

I had to stop suddenly." I put my arms around her. "I love you, Des. I will take you anyplace you want to go, but I need for you to be safe. I think we should plan our big trip in September for my 50th Birthday."

She smiled. "I've been thinking about that. How about taking a cruise to Alaska"?

"Sounds like a great trip. That will give you something to look forward to in your down time." I placed my hand gently on her left chest area. "Speaking of looking forward to something, are you ready to look at this incision? We need to change the bandage anyway."

Des nodded, and we walked into the bathroom. She sat on the chair facing the mirror. I gently removed the top bandage that covered the incision and removed it, revealing a puffy incision held together with staples.

Her right hand moved to touch the staples. Tears erupted and streamed down her cheeks. "It's so ugly." She whispered.

"No, it's not," I responded. "It's a beautiful reminder that you are alive because of this scar." I cupped her chin in my hands. "I'll remember each time I see that scar, that the cancer was discovered in time and we have a life together because the cancer is gone. It's a beautiful scar honey, and you are a beautiful woman. You don't need to have two breasts to be the woman I love." I kissed her gently on the lips, and from one end of the incision to the other. "It doesn't make any difference to me, and I know you feel like a great part of you has been cut away, but that will change in time. You are more than your breasts."

She looked up at me through teary eyes. "I hope they got it all."

"Me too," I whispered.

"I feel so betrayed by my body. I don't feel like I can ever trust it again" Her words trailed off to a low whisper.

"We just need to trust the Lord. He has our futures scheduled, and what will be, will be His will." I bandaged the wound and stood for a long time with my arms around her.

We had planned on forever being a lot of years together, and now it seemed that each day was our forever. We needed to learn how to live each day as if it were the last, because the fear of those little cancer cells were always on our minds.

Two weeks later, the tubes were removed, and the staples were removed. I don't know why, but I kept the staples and the surgical clamp remover as a reminder of what Des had gone through.

Two weeks after that, we arrived at the oncology office to begin a six month treatment of chemotherapy. It took between two and three hours for the medicine drip, and I took off work for each treatment. That first time is seared into my memory.

We went into a large room lined with about a dozen recliners. Des sat in a huge brown leather recliner, with her right arm resting on a padded shelf. We had learned already to guard her left arm from any injections or blood draws. There would always be the possibility of lymph swelling due to the surgery having been on her left side.

The nurse brought in the combination of chemo drugs, (CMF) and hung them on the stand beside the chair. A maze of tubing would allow a slow drip to mix the drugs and feed them into the vein on the top of Des' hand.

We watched the process, as the nurse stuck the needle into her vein then taped it to her skin. Des looked up at the little bags, then looked at me, and began to cry.

"Does it hurt"? I asked concerned. My eyes filled with tears.

She shook her head to indicate, "No". So much emotion was pent up as she experienced the first of many injections. My heart was breaking. *Please God, let this kill off all the cells.*

Every two weeks for the next six months, we went through the same procedure. Des would suffer nausea, and pain in her bones along with exhaustion. She lost her hair, and opted to wear hats and scarves instead of a wig. The scar had healed fine and each visit to the oncologist was encouraging. The tumor was small, and the lymph nodes were not involved, so the chemo was "just in case" there were cancer cells elsewhere in the body.

Everyone was confident that the cancer was gone, and after the chemo treatments, she would only have to come in every six months for follow up blood tests.

"Five years seems to be the magic number" we were assured by nurses and doctors who examined her. "If you make it without a reoccurrence, then you are truly a survivor."

A vital part of Des' recovery was her first trip to be fitted with prosthesis and the special bras designed to hold the breast. We were referred to Bras for Body and Soul located in Fremont California. We were introduced to Tricia McMahon who is the founder of the boutique and the HERS Breast Cancer Foundation. Des and Tricia bonded almost immediately and when we left the store I noticed a slight smile.

"Does it feel weird to have a breast there again"? I asked.

"It feels heavy." She responded. "I was just wondering if anyone can tell that it's not my real breast."

"It looks real enough to me." I grinned. "No one else should be looking that close."

Tricia had taken time to get the right fit, and had advised Des that it would take awhile to get used to both the bra and the silicone breast.

Her incision was still tender, and it would be a few weeks until wearing the bra would be totally comfortable.

Des finished her last chemotherapy treatment just before our cruise in September. She was feeling stronger and had returned to a limited schedule of work. We took several short trips, mostly to the ocean. As the months were turned on the calendar, we found new events to celebrate. Her hair grew back darker and with more curls than ever. Not only did we continue to celebrate our monthly anniversary of being together, but we added a night out to celebrate one more month cancer free.

One day Des and I were talking about how our attitude toward life had changed. She said, "I no longer take things for granted. If today is all I have, I want to enjoy my life and continue to grow in the Lord." Her eyes were blinking back tears as she reached out and took my hand. "I wanted to grow old with you and travel after you retired. Now, I just want to travel, and have you use your vacation days each year. I want us to keep taking short trips and some longer ones while we can."

"I can take time whenever you want, Des." I looked at her a long time before I spoke again. "Do you have the feeling that our time is short?"

"I don't know Darlene. I just don't want to miss out on anything." We embraced in silence, afraid to speak the doubts that lived just below the surface of our happiness.

"You know, I've been attending this support group from Kaiser for women with breast cancer. The stories I hear just break my heart. Most of their husbands are less than supportive, and several have gone through divorce since they had surgery. One woman had a reoccurrence and it's been almost ten years since her initial cancer."

"What happened to the five year cut off"? I questioned.

"I think that is just wishful thinking." The more I find out about breast cancer, the more convinced I am that you will be a survivor as long as you live, but you only live as long as God let's you live."

"I'm praying that will be a long, long time!" I tried to lighten the mood. "We still have places to go and sunsets to see!"

"Speaking of that, I've made reservations at our timeshare in Mexico for next month! You need to schedule vacation time."

"Just let me know the dates!" I was happy to have Des make the vacation plans. I enjoyed being anywhere in the world with her, and I wanted to go where she would be happy.

"Oh, something else I forgot to tell you. I've been asked to take part in a breast cancer case study. I have one meeting a month, and each week a nurse will call to fill out a questionnaire on life patterns. I figure if I can help someone by what I've gone through, then I will participate."

"That sounds great honey. I think it is good to share your story with other women at support groups. I know that not all of them are women of faith."

"Not only that, Darlene. Most of the women don't have a partner who supports them and encourages them the way you do. I tell them about our relationship and how blessed I am to have a Christian Partner."

"Well, I can imagine how much emotional pain they go through to have their husband reject them because of losing a breast. Cancer is bad enough but rejection from a spouse is terrible." I put my arms around her and held her close. "Des, I promise you that no matter what happens in our future, I will never abandon you and I will be here for you. I will take care of you for all of our lives, in sickness and in health, and until death do us part, even if we can't get married!"

"Maybe someday we will be able to have a ceremony and invite our friends." She paused, "Darlene, I'm more married to you than I ever was to John."

"Marriage isn't what's written on a piece of paper, it's a commitment of heart, life, past and future. I am married to you, Des, and no ceremony can make that more real."

Most of our conversations involved Breast Cancer survivors, with new reports almost monthly of someone in the group who was diagnosed again with cancer somewhere in their body. It might be the lung, liver or bones, but it was still the primary breast cancer cells. Each time we heard of another woman having cancer, or each time we attended a funeral for one of the members of Des' support group, we wondered if Des was really healed. The women were as young as twenty and several were in their seventies. Cancer was no respecter of age.

We joined the Breast Cancer Action group, and Des had a hat that read, "Cancer Sucks". I wore it when we would walk in support of all women with Breast Cancer. Our life seemed to be balanced between church events; visiting women who were too sick to come to her support group. Des felt led to pray with complete strangers at times, and share her cancer journey. When we could, we took vacations.

My job that had occupied my life for almost thirty years was now secondary in importance. I wanted to be with Des, rather than at the office. Some days I would call in sick and spend the day with her on her uniform routes. I was amazed at the nurses who would come out to the van just to talk, even if they didn't buy any new uniforms. Des shared her faith and often prayed with them about problems in their lives. She had her own ministry that grew with her openness about her bout with cancer. I was blessed to be part of her emotional and spiritual support.

Des' patience and continued outreach to her sons had also changed their relationships. Both sons had come to visit with her on several occasions, and they were able to talk about why she needed to leave the marriage. Phillip was especially sensitive and said that he was glad she was happy now, and commented that even his dad could move on with his life. Nathan seemed a bit more stand offish. However Des continued to include him in our special celebrations. She took him on several trips, and we agreed to pray that God would change his heart and heal his wounded spirit.

It had been about four and a half years since her surgery. My health plan had changed at work and I was able to add Des as my domestic partner and move her from Kaiser Insurance to my medical insurance. Our premiums were cheaper, and she had better access to specialty doctors.

It was July 2001 and we were off on another short trip. My niece was getting married in Denver, and we wanted to be present for her event. Des and I flew to New Mexico and drove up to Colorado on back roads, enjoying the scenery and the farm land. We spent several days in the area, then drove back to Albuquerque and flew home. Des was feeling tired in the weeks after our trip and seemed to be having difficulty taking deep breaths.

She went to the doctor and they took a chest x-ray and ran blood tests. It was suspected that she had mononucleosis and was advised to rest. By mid August, she wasn't any better and after some research on the internet, the doctor felt that she might have Valley Fever. It could have been picked up through spores in the soil on our trip through the Midwest.

The tests proved inconclusive. She was increasingly exhausted and hardly able to make it through her daily appointments. We had a trip to Maui planned for my birthday in September. The doctor advised against going, as Des was beginning to run a fever on a daily basis. Her breathing was labored at times, and she felt like there was a pressure in her lungs. Our trip to Hawaii was a week away.

"We don't have to go, Des. We can cancel it and put you in the hospital until they figure out what is wrong with you."

"No, I want to go. I can feel just as bad in Hawaii as I can at home." She grinned. "I might even feel better on the beach."

"It's up to you, Des. I don't like the feel of this. Whatever is wrong needs to be identified and treated." I was anxious about the high fever each morning.

"Maybe it's that bird flu that I had last year from that diseased parakeet." She sounded more hopeful. "I just want to go to Hawaii again."

"Ok, honey. I just want you to get over this fever."

"I'll be fine," she assured me. "The doctor says my liver count is a little high and wants to run more tests, but we can wait until we're back home."

We arrived in Hawaii and checked into our condo. Des wanted to go swimming in the ocean, so we made our way to a secluded beach area. She walked out with the waves hitting her at waist level. "Come on in," she called to me.

I walked out to join her. "The water is really warm, it feels good."

"You think the water is warm"? she questioned. "I feel really cold."

I looked at her face, and then touched her skin. She was clammy. "I think we better get you back to the room." I guided her back to shore.

By the time we reached the room and took her temperature, it was 103. I gave her some Tylenol and began to wipe her down with a wash cloth.

She looked scared. "I think you better get me to a hospital."

"Really"? I wasn't sure she was serious.

"Yes, Darlene"! She yelled at me. "There is something seriously wrong here."

I bundled her up and drove to the top of the island where I had seen hospital signs. We drove into Emergency and by that time she was burning hot. I gave all of her medical history to the intake nurse. They had her stand and put her right leg behind her. The pain was so intense, she almost passed out.

"I think you have appendicitis" the nurse stated. We need to take some x-rays and get you prepped for surgery.

They wheeled her away for x-rays and I walked outside to use my cell phone. I called her parents to let them know Des was in the hospital. I told them I would let them know as soon as we had some answers.

A half hour later I checked with the nursing station and got permission to go into ER where Des was being held. She was just finishing a drink so they could do a CT scan.

"The X-rays were clear." She looked upset. "They were all set to operate and I told them not until something shows on the film."

"So, what are they trying to find on the CT scan"?

"There's got to be a source of this pain and fever!" She started to cry. "I guess I shouldn't have made this trip."

"Don't worry about it Des. If you have to have surgery for something, I'll change the tickets and we'll fly back to California! This is really stupid that the doctors are not able to identify a problem. You don't have these symptoms for no reason!" I took her hand. "We'll get it figured out honey."

"I hope so." She grimaced with pain. "I don't know how much more of this I can handle."

"Have they given you anything for pain"?

"No, they want to do the CT scan first." Just then an orderly came and wheeled her away.

I waited another 45 minutes. The same orderly brought her back to the room.

"Well"? I questioned.

"Nothing showed up on the scan. We'll be releasing her with some pain medication."

Des was in tears. "I don't know what to do," she said quietly.

"We'll take you back to the condo and if things aren't better in the morning, I'm taking you back to Hayward."

It was almost 4 A.M. when we were cleared to leave. I drove to the south side of the island to our condo. Once Des was in bed, I went to the front room and called her folks again. "I don't know if we will come home early or stay for the week. I'm just going to let her sleep as long as she can, and keep giving her pain pills."

They asked that I keep them informed, and I promised I would do that.

The next two days Des stayed in bed taking pain pills and trying to keep from being nauseated. The third day, she decided to go to the local urgent care center. That doctor diagnosed an intestinal bacterium, and gave her antibiotics, and more pain pills. She spent the rest of the week in bed. Our week in Maui was over, and Des felt bad that my birthday celebration had been spent trying to get her well. My only concern was to get her home and check in with our doctor. I stopped by Maui Memorial and picked up copies of all the tests they had performed, so we wouldn't have to repeat them. The trip home was uneventful, but my concern was growing with each passing day. Once we were home, I made an appointment for Des later that week. I was hoping for some results from the tests she had taken before our trip.

Early the next morning, Des woke me up. "These pain pills are not even touching this pain." She was having trouble breathing, and could hardly sit up. "You need to get me to the hospital,"

"Should I call 911"? I rushed to put on my clothes.

"No, you can drive me there faster than waiting for them." She pulled her robe around her shoulders and tried to stand. She was burning up with fever.

I put my arm around her waist and helped her to the car. We pulled into the ER room in less than 5 minutes. I ran in and yelled for someone to come help me. Two nurses came with a wheel chair, and we began the information process.

Four hours later, they once again released her. The diagnosis was dehydration and hyperventilation due to anxiety. They thought the antibiotics she received in Hawaii would work in time, and recommended she see her doctor at the end of the week.

I was angry. "What is causing the high fever? Just look at her, this is not just anxiety!"

The duty nurse was patient. "All the tests were negative. There is nothing further we can do at this time."

I took Des home and kept her drugged with pain medication. Two days later, we kept the doctor appointment with Dr. Patel. I brought all the paperwork from three trips to the ER and the results of two chest x-rays and one CT scan.

"There is something terribly wrong here. Someone has to be able to figure out what is going on with her body. Can we go to UCSF and see a specialist? This waiting game just isn't working for us any longer" I was very upset, but tried to keep my voice at a normal pitch.

"The doctor reviewed the reports. "I'm at a total loss to understand what is wrong with you." She looked at Des. "My suggestion is to have you admitted to the hospital and let them run tests until someone figures out this mystery. The fastest way to have that happen is to wheel you over to ER from here and go in on an emergency basis. Tell them you are not leaving until you have a diagnosis that makes sense." She turned to address me. "Darlene, I am as frustrated as you are, and we need to get Des diagnosed. Let's give this one more try."

"We will do whatever it takes." I responded. "Do I put her in a wheelchair and push her to the Emergency room"?

"No. I'll have one of our office girls do that, and I'll call over there and tell them to expect her."

Within minutes we were once again going through her medical history and the Doctor on call came into the room.

"Hello. My name is Dr. Garcia. I have read the reports and I know you are pretty upset with not knowing what's going on with your body. I am having you admitted to the hospital and we will figure things out. I want to rerun the blood tests, and do another MRI to rule out more obvious causes."

I was able to stay with Des while they processed her admission to the hospital. I went with her to the room, and waited while they took her to X-ray, and the room to do a new CT scan. I stayed until 10 PM when they insisted I leave for the night and return the next morning. My heart felt like it was breaking as I leaned down to kiss her good-bye. "I'll be here first thing in the morning," I whispered in her ear. "Call me during the night if you need to talk."

It was about eight A.M. when I made my way into the hospital room. Des was propped up with pillows, hooked to IV's and had her eyes closed. I came over to the bed. and took her hand. "Are you alright Des"?

She opened her eyes and stared at me. The curtains in the room were drawn and it was not real bright. I saw the tears streaming down her cheeks. "I just had a vision." Her voice was so low I had to lean forward to hear her words."

"What kind of vision"? I asked.

"There have been so many doctors in and out of here all night. At first I wasn't sure if this was real, or an actual vision. The room was dark and I was just lying here. The door opened and a doctor came in with my file. He opened it and asked, "Are you Mrs. Lambson?" Then, he read from the paperwork and said, "You have a metastases breast cancer. We're going to do what we can to make you better." He closed the file and left the room.

'Then, almost immediately the door opened and another male figure walked in. I couldn't see His face. He had a thick file in his hands.

"Hello Des", he said. "I know who you are. I know what is wrong with you and I know what is going to happen to you. Be at Peace." He opened the file in his hands and turned it toward me. Across the top in black bold letters it read **"Forgiven."** Across the bottom it read **BE AT PEACE.** He closed the file and walked out of the room."

"It was the Lord," I whispered.

She nodded. The tears were a constant stream down her cheeks. "Now I know what the problem is with my body."

Cancer never entered my mind. It was almost five years, and no sign of cancer had shown up in any of her tests.

I reached down and held her while our tears mingled with our sobs. We didn't hear the door open when Dr. Garcia came into the room.

He had a file in his hands. "I have the results of the tests. It took some time, but we found a spot on your left lung where your breast cancer has returned. It's a stage four cancer, however we can treat it with chemotherapy."

Des cleared her throat. "I already knew that was the problem. The Lord came to me in a vision and gave me the news this morning."

Dr .Garcia looked surprised. "I believe in Him too, so that doesn't shock me. Now that we know what it is, let's get a plan of treatment. I'll have the oncologist come speak with you." He left the room.

I held her hand, my gut feeling like I had just been kicked. "I'm so sorry Des. I wish this were happening to me, instead of you."

"It's happening to both of us," she said softly. "You know Darlene; it's four years and eleven months."

Chapter Six
Fighting the Battle- Living with Dying

Now that we knew what it was, we needed to find out how to treat it, and what that would actually mean to our lives.

What we did know for sure is that there was a tumor in her left lung and they wanted to do a biopsy in order to determine that it was metastases of her original breast cancer and not a new primary. They scheduled her for the procedure at UCSF Medical Center as they had more experience than our local hospital. Our insurance group assigned a case worker to handle the red tape for her medical care. We came to appreciate Kathy as a friend and not just someone who would schedule tests and deal with all medical approvals.

On the day of the lung biopsy, Des' mother and father drove up from southern California to provide emotional support. Des was still weak from the fever and pain, and had only been out of the hospital for two days. We drove to San Francisco and found parking near the emergency entrance. I found a wheel chair and brought it to the car, as she was not able to walk even the short distance to admittance.

I was able to stay with her through all the preparations for this surgical procedure. The more details we received, the more frightened I became. They had taken a new MRI and knew the exact location of the tumor. It was millimeters from her heart and the process would entail inserting a small rod with a needle inside to puncture the tumor and suck out the tissue for a biopsy. They would not put her under, but would use local anesthetic to perform the surgical task, and it was dangerous. We were told it could puncture the heart lining. She had to sign waivers and understand the risk before they could do the surgery. The doctors had to determine the type of cancer before they could start chemo treatments, so our options were limited.

We waited in the pre-op room and I held her hand. I leaned close to her ear as she lay with her eyes closed.

I prayed the first of many prayers. "Heavenly Father, Des is your daughter. Please give the doctors steady hands and help us both not to be afraid. We trust you for her life, and all of our tomorrows. Please give us both peace for this day. In Jesus Name, I ask it. Amen." I kissed her cheek. "I love you, Des and we will get through this test, and all the others that we need to go through to get you well."

She opened her eyes. "Thank you for praying," she whispered. "I love you too."

They came and wheeled her into the operating room, and my eyes filled with tears.

Help me be strong for her, Lord. I will die if she doesn't make it through this. I walked out to the waiting room and joined her parents. "We have about an hour, so let's go to the cafeteria and have some coffee.

I explained the process to them while we had coffee and a donut. I looked at her dad. "I feel so helpless. I love Des so much and would do anything in the world for her, and all I can do is pray."

Her mother reached over and patted my hand. "You're a good friend Darlene. She wouldn't be able to handle this if you weren't there for her. We appreciate you so much."

Dad chimed in. "We know you do a lot for her Darlene. We do appreciate the fact that you are here for her and take care of her. We are so far away and can only be here some of the time. You are a good friend."

"She's my very best friend," I murmured. "I'm still in shock that the cancer came back after all this time." Then it occurred to me. *The cancer didn't come back; it's been there all the time and just took this long to grow large enough to be detected.*

We talked for an hour, and then went back to the waiting room. I checked with the nurse, who told me they would have Des in recovery in just a few minutes. She told me the procedure was successful, and that we would have the results within 48 hours. She told me that Des had to be still for an hour or so before we could take her home, but that we could come in and visit with her.

We walked into the recovery room and Des was on the gurney in a corner slot. Her eyes were closed. Her gown was pulled to the side and I could see a gauze bandage taped to her chest.

"How are you feeling"? I asked, taking her hand in mine.

"Like hell," she whispered. "That was the most scary thing I've ever had done to my body."

"Were you awake for the whole thing"?

"Yes, I had to be in order to inhale and exhale so they could go right to the tumor." She paused. "They inserted a rod through my chest wall and into my lung. I could taste the blood in my throat. The rod was real thin, and as my heart was beating, the rod was moving back and forth with each beat! It was scary to think they were that close to the wall of my heart and could slip and nick my heart! I was really praying."

"I was too, honey. I'm glad you are finished with this test. They said they got the sample, and we should have results within 48 hours."

It seemed like forever until the doctor came out and signed her release form. We were free to take Des back home, and wait another day for the results. We had an appointment with the oncology staff in two days to review videos that would explain the new chemotherapy treatments and get us on a regular schedule. There were so many appointments and so much new information that I carried a notebook to write down information and questions that we wanted to ask. Once more, our world was going to revolve around treatments that may or may not work against the cancer.

Des' mother and dad stayed one more day before returning to their home in southern California. We were alone and able to process the weeks events.

"This is going to be a very busy week, and I'm sure an emotional one." I took her hand as we sat on the loveseat in our front room. "Once we get the schedule for chemo, I'll arrange to take time off work to go with you to the appointments."

"I want you to be there for the first one, but I think we can work out something with Sandy and Becky. Sandy has Friday off from her job and Becky is not working right now, so she would be available. I don't want you to miss a lot of time off work." She reached out and took my hand. "God has placed some special women in our lives. I know that our church will be there to support both of us any way they can."

"Honey, you are my top priority. I have plenty of vacation time and comp time to cover the days you will need to receive your chemo treatments." I paused. "I really want to be with you."

"I know that Darlene. We don't know how long this is going to go on, and we will need our friends to be part of our healing process. I was thinking of something else. I'm going to ask the doctor to authorize having a permanent port installed in my chest so that I don't have to go through the problem of a nurse not being able to hit my vein each time."

"How does a port work"? I asked.

"They do a major surgical procedure to install a titanium tube in my chest that is inserted into the heart valve and has an opening just under my skin. When the needle is inserted into the tube, they go through my skin with a small prick, and it is so much better than having I/V tubes taped to my hand. They can also do blood draws through that tube and I know that will work a lot better. My veins are collapsing from the chemotherapy I had the first time."

"Let's get it done then. We can call Kathy at the health center and she will get the paperwork approved." I stroked her arm. "I'm so sorry that the cancer came back Des. I really thought that we were going to beat the statistics."

"I did too." She whispered. "But I know one thing. If God chooses to heal me, He has the power to do that. If He chooses to take me home, then my healing will be complete there. I'm going to live every day knowing that whatever happens is God's plan for my life. I want to live boldly for Him, and if that means having cancer, then so be it."

Just then, the phone rang. I picked up the receiver. "Hello"

"This is Doctor Garcia. Is this Des"?

"No, this is Darlene. Just a moment please." I handed her the phone and glanced at my watch. It was 6:30 P.M.

"Hello. This is Des." Her voice was shaky.

"I don't usually call to give this sort of news, but I know you've been waiting to hear the results of your biopsy. I just got the report from UCSF. They have confirmed that the cells are from your original cancer, so this is metastases of breast cancer, and not lung cancer. The breast cancer cells can show up anywhere in the body. We will treat this tumor aggressively, and see if we can slow down the progression." He paused. "Des, this is stage 4, and you are classified as terminal. We might be able to slow it down, but in the long run, this will be what will terminate your life."

Tears were running down Des' cheeks. "Is there a time frame for this to happen"?

"Only God knows the hour of our death, Des. I'm a doctor and can only give you information based upon my experience. It depends on how well your body responds to the chemotherapy. There are three or four new drugs on the market, and our best hope is that this cancer will respond well to the treatments. You have a good attitude and that's a big part of the battle. I know you are going to fight with all you have, and we as your doctors will help you with the battle. I want you to come into the office tomorrow and we'll go over details."

Des hung up the phone, choking back sobs. "I don't want to die. There is too much to do yet."

I held her in my arms. "You're not going to die yet; we'll take it one day at a time." That night, like so many to follow was filled with conversations on how to fight the cancer and not let it consume our relationship. I remembered hearing someone say, "You've got to live until you die", and that became important to us.

The treatments began in December, 2001. Des had the port-o-cath installed on December 6th, and her first treatment was on the 8th. The schedule was every two weeks for six months. After three months, they would do a CT scan to see if the tumor was shrinking, and determine further treatments based upon those results.

Des began to feel better within weeks of the first treatment. Her fever stabilized at a normal of 99.0 and her exhaustion seemed to fade away. Once again she lost her hair and had to take booster shots to replenish her white cells. Her immune system was compromised and we needed to be cautious about being in public places. I had to limit visitors during this crucial time, but encouraged our friends to call on the phone and talk and pray with Des. Our network of friends was a lifeline to the hope that cancer would not rob us of Christian fellowship.

A new form of ministry was opening for Des at the oncology office. There was space for five or six clients at a time, and the infusions would take several hours. Des began to talk with the other men and women who were receiving chemo treatments. They shared experiences with side effects, talked about family, and new treatments. When a new person joined the room, Des always introduced herself and spoke of her faith in the Lord Jesus. Many of the women would ask her to pray with them for their families and for peace in their lives. Two of the nurses were Christians, and although they usually did not join in the conversations, they always listened to Des share encouragement with others.

I remember one young woman in particular who always came with her two young daughters. She had been a teacher, and this was her second occurrence with breast cancer. Her girls would color or do school projects while they waited with their mother. She talked openly about her chances of recovery and how difficult it would be for her husband to raise the girls. This young woman did not respond well to the chemo treatments and each session made it more obvious that she was losing her battle. The last time we saw her; Des went over to her and asked if she could pray with her. The woman agreed, and Des prayed softly for peace and direction for their family. When the woman left that day I remember Des saying quietly. "I'll see you in heaven." It broke my heart and I couldn't hold back the tears. *It's not fair God to take a young mother and leave her kids to wonder what kind of God allowed her to die.* My thoughts were jarred by Des touching my knee. "It's all right Darlene. She is ready to go, and God will take care of her daughters." Des' faith was simple, and it was strong. I was the one asking questions because I would also be the one left to deal with grief.

The weeks passed, and when the new CT was taken, it showed that the spot on her lungs had almost disappeared. They would complete the six month course of chemotherapy, and keep our fingers crossed that all the cancer cells would be gone. Sandy and Becky were alternating weeks to take her to the treatments so that I would not have to miss work. My immediate supervisor made frequent comments about my job being the top priority. I was very stressed over not being able to be with Des, but greatly relieved that I could rely on our church family to meet our needs.

Several major events occurred in early 2002 that changed our lives more than the cancer diagnosis. My company sent me to Nevada to train some new hires. The regulations in Nevada differ from California, and I was not as familiar with the products. The two weeks I spent training the new employees did not go well, and complaints were made to my supervisor. Within two weeks of my return to San Francisco, I was called in for an interview to see what action would be taken against me. I was in shock when I was told that this could cost me my job. I had 36 years in with AAA, and had thought I would work for them until I retired years from now. On a Friday night, just before I left the office, I received a misdirected email with an attachment written by my supervisor. The facts were taken out of context and they were framed in such a way as to present a case for termination. The email was to human resources, but it had come to me instead. I called my supervisor and presented her with the errors, and asked if they were in fact going to terminate me the following Monday. She said that was true. I registered my intent to retire immediately. I couldn't take a chance on losing coverage for Des and her coverage for the cancer treatments. Within an hour I had packed up my desk and ended my career with AAA. I called Des in tears, but overwhelming peace swept over me when she reminded me that now, we would be able to have quality time together. She said; "Remember where the Bible says, what was intended for evil, God intended for good. He knew you would never leave that company on your own. He also knows that I need you to be with me, and this will work out"!

It was a major transition and I spent several months in therapy talking about my feelings and the direction of our life. In the end, I'm grateful to be retired and I know it was for the best.

The other major change came as Des realized that she was not able continue with her uniform business. The weight of the uniform bins was too much for her body. My sister, Debbie who lived in Washington State had recently opened a uniform business. We made some calls and Debbie agreed to purchase all existing inventory as well as the Delivery van. Des and I made a trip up north and delivered everything to her. We spent a few days visiting, and then flew home to California.

We now had the freedom to take camping trips, go visiting with family and friends at will, as long as Des' strength continued to increase.

We attended several breast cancer conferences to keep informed on new treatments and resources. Des was an avid reader and felt that the more information she had, the better prepared she was for the journey ahead. Her second great love was for music, and she would spend hours listening to worship CD's and singing praise choruses. At one of the breast cancer conferences, we met a woman named Beth Baker who had come from Oregon to provide music for the conference. Each song on her album ministered to us, but one in particular seemed written just for us.

We live on Borrowed Time*

I never thought that there could be, a love like yours and mine.
I never dreamed that I would see the day that I would find,
A love that feels so right,
But here we are tonight,
And now the only thing we really need is time.

We live on borrowed time,
No one can be sure when the loan will finally come due
But I'm loving all of life-
I know what time is for; I borrowed it so I could spend it all right here with you.

There was a time when I believed that life held guarantees
There was a time when I was sure my future was secure;
But life had other plans,
The future's in Gods hands…
Knowing that has let me live and love you more
We live on borrowed time,
Yesterday is past-
Tomorrow seems a million miles away.
But I promise you that I'm going to make love last,
By living every moment; every hour of every day…
And we may have a year; and we may have a lifetime.
No one can be certain what the future will allow.
You and I are here, and this time is the right time.
One thing that I know is that we have each other now——
And now—-
We live on borrowed time. Let's celebrate and sing as we walk bravely into the
Unknown—-cause we're going to be just fine; whatever life may bring

We'll face it all together, and we'll never be alone
We may not have forever-
But our time will be our own.
Vocal by Beth Baker on I've got to sing my Song. Lyrics by David Freidman @ Midder 2000. Used by Permission.

When Des and I left that conference, we knew this was our new song. We had been making plans to have a commitment ceremony in January 2003, and this song would be one that we sang to each other. Des would be turning 50 that month, and we were planning our ten year "wedding' to mark that event as well as take a special trip to Niagara Falls.

The cancer faded into the back of our minds as more months passed without any new symptoms. Our commitment ceremony was set to happen in January 2003 at a resort by the Napa River. My sister Arlene and her husband Charlie were planning on attending from Washington State. Des' son Phillip was also making plans to be present to support our public commitment. Phillip was now in his early twenties and had reconciled with his mother after her divorce from John. Her older son, Nathan, was still angry, and we did not expect him to attend our celebration. There would be dozens of church family and friends from my work place. Sandy, Cherie and Becky were there to help with food and emotional support. Becky had worked as a caterer and we knew she would help make the day an event to remember. Each of our friends would have a special role in the ceremony. Our guest list included straight, gay, Christian, non-Christian, Buddhists, Catholics and Baptists. Our friend and former pastor Howard agreed to perform the ceremony.

Two days before the event, Des started running a fever. By the day of the wedding, she was running 105 temperatures, and I had to give her alcohol sponge baths to try and break the fever. We had a flight out to the East coast leaving early the next morning.

In addition to the high temperature, Des began to experience severe bone pain in her ribs and in her hips. Her energy level was low, but she was determined to see the Niagara Falls, and we arranged our days to allow plenty of rest. We knew the cancer was back One week would not make a difference in the treatment. Once again, her doctors recommended that she not take the trip, but Des was insistent. We were leaving and would and trust God with the end results.

Our commitment ceremony was beautiful and everyone helped with the set up and the reception that followed. Des had to sit for part of the ceremony, but managed to stand for our vows. We had everyone bring flowers to decorate the arch, under which we stood. It was a symbol of the family and community we embraced.

Our reception was flawless, as everyone worked together to decorate and handle the food. Des' son handled the barbeque; while others pitched in for music and decorations. About half way through the event, Des had to go to our room and lay down but even then, friends went to stay with her so she was included in the celebration.

Our friend Becky brought special champagne flutes and after the majority of guests had departed, we gathered for a private toast. Our closest friends not only gathered to wish us well, but prayed for our safety and Des' strength to handle the trip.

My determination to see that Des would be able to make the trip was greater than my fear that she might die while we were gone. We had friends drop us off at the airport and our honeymoon trip became a reality.

Each night I would whisper, "We live on borrowed time...we're going to be just fine."

Des would respond. "Whatever life may bring, we'll face it all together-We'll never be alone. We may not have forever, but our time will be our own." Each day we lived knowing that we would never be back to this place and we needed to burn the memories into our brains, so we could remember good times.

On the morning that we were leaving to return home, we stopped for breakfast at a restaurant on Cape Cod. Part way through our meal, Des remembered that she had left something at the motel, and asked me to drive back and retrieve it. I knew that we had plenty of time to make our flight, so I left her at the restaurant.

When I returned about 15 minutes later, I found her sitting in the booth with tears running down her cheeks.

"What's wrong, honey"? I asked as I slipped in beside her.

Her right hand was grasping something in a fist. She opened her hand and showed me a small medal that was flat on one side, and had an angel on the other. "Do you remember the two women who were sitting in front of us when you left"?

"Not really," I responded. 'Why"?

"I overheard them talking about California. I started up a conversation, and come to find out one of the women lived in the Bay Area, and was a nurse." She paused. "I shared with them about my cancer journey." The tears were flowing freely now, and she brushed them away. "They were Christians. The nurse gave me this angel medal and told me she would be praying for me, and if I ever doubted that God was with me, to just look at the medal and remember this time."

"Wow." I whispered softly. "That's really a special gift from the Lord! We know that people all over the country are praying for your healing."

I hugged her and kissed her cheek. "You have angels watching over you all the time!"

The flight home was filled with uncertainty about new tests and treatments, but neither of us had regrets at taking this trip. God had made his presence known many times throughout the week, and we braced ourselves for the days ahead.

The following week, new bone scans and an MRI revealed that the cancer had returned and was present in her ribs; in her hips and in one area on her clavicle bone. It had been just over a year since the breast cancer had invaded her lungs. In addition to a new round of chemotherapy, she would undergo radiation treatments on her hips, as they were the support bones and were the most involved in her ability to walk. The rib cage could respond to the chemotherapy treatments.

The radiation was designed to target specific areas on the hip and pelvis, and was scheduled over a 12 week time period. The treatment itself was painless, but the radiation began to leave skin burns. I would cut a leaf from our Aloe Vera plant, split it open and cover her burns with the sticky substance on the inside. It seemed to help the burns, and soothe the areas that were radiated. Des was using a walker with a seat in order to walk any distance at all. She was determined to fight the effects of both the radiation and the chemotherapy. Each treatment depended upon white cell counts or red cell counts, both of which were treated with additional shots of chemicals to boost the numbers. As the months passed, her cancer seemed to be responding to the treatments, and once again we were hopeful that God was granting us more time together.

Additional Pet Scans, MRI's and X-Rays seemed to indicate that the cancer was put into remission once again, and we resumed a schedule that didn't include a doctor's visit each week. We made a trip to Washington to visit with my family and spent a week at a resort on the beach. Des could no longer walk long distances or swim, but I would drive her to the shore and set up a chair. She would sit for hours and watch the waves, listening to the gulls and singing worship songs. Life was lived on pain pills and morphine patches, but we were able to travel.

Our trips changed to train or plane, so that she would not have to sit for long periods of time. We returned to our timeshare in Mexico for a week, traveling with friends who could help me with her care. She insisted on being in the water, and since I couldn't swim, I would send our friend Sandy to watch over her. I was determined to help her enjoy all places that brought her happiness, and the water was one place I couldn't join her. We took a cruise to the Caribbean with her parents and her son Phillip. They had several water adventures that brought

Des much happiness. Phillip was able to watch her in the water and if need be, to bring her to shore when she didn't have the strength to make it on her own. Life was not quite normal, but it was a time for making memories.

In May of 2004 we were able to take a trip by train to Canada, and across to Edmonton. We picked up a rental car, and began a trip to see Banff and Lake Louise. We would travel short distances and allow for Des to rest. She was using a walker and once again, was determined to see places we had never traveled.

I remember being in a cabin by the river in British Columbia. We were sitting on the small deck, looking out over the most beautiful valley with a river that seemed to go on forever. Des reached over and took my hand.

"Thank you for bringing me on this trip." She squeezed my fingers. "I was just thinking, what would happen if I died while we were on this trip."

"Don't even think about that Des. I would get you home one way or another." I smiled. "God isn't through with us yet."

She looked at me very intently. "I think what is more fearful, is what I would do if you died while we were up here. I can't even walk to the car or drive without your help."

"Well, I don't intend to die in the near future. If something happened to me, you would call Debbie and Quin and they would come get us and take care of the situation."

"Would they do that in a foreign country"? She was serious.

"Yes, they would take care of us," I assured her. "However, we don't need to think about that happening. I'm not sick and I'll take care of you myself."

"I just hate feeling so helpless, Darlene. You have to do all the work and it's not fair."

I moved closer to her and held her in my arms. "We may not have forever honey, but no one is keeping track of what's fair. Life is what it is, and we're living each day, together."

Our trip was not without moments of pain, both emotional and physical for Des, but we made the journey with a lot of beautiful pictures of wildlife, and many talks late into the night about God's grace. We spoke of life and death, and how we were facing each of those events, knowing that when the time of separation came, there would be the strength to survive.

Des continued to share her story and her faith with people who crossed our path. One event stands out more than any other. We had gone to brunch at a restaurant over- looking the ocean. Des was still using her walker to assist her in going long distances. I placed the walker next to the wall by our table.

"I'll go through the line and bring you back a plate of great sea food." I grinned. "You know I can hardly stand the smell of fishy stuff, but for you anything"!

I was gone for about five minutes. When I returned I noticed that Des looked pale and seemed to be struggling to breathe. "What's wrong"? I asked, as I sat her plate down in front of her. "Are you ok"?

She looked up at me and whispered. "God just spoke to me." She took a deep breath and continued. "He told me to go talk to that woman across from us and give her a message."

I turned my head to see the couple across the aisle. "Well, you better go do it then."

"Really"? She seemed a little hesitant. "What if I heard God wrong"?

"I think you heard Him perfectly." I whispered. "Do you want your walker"?

"No." She stood slowly and made her way to the table.

I closed my eyes and began to pray silently. *Lord please give her the boldness and the wisdom and let her be received as an ambassador from You.*

I couldn't hear the conversation, but after a couple of minutes, the young woman stood to her feet and gave Des a hug. I heard her say "Thank you so much." And then she sat back down.

Des returned to her seat, her eyes were filled with tears. "It was the right thing" she whispered. "I told her I didn't usually do things like this, but that I had cancer and I wouldn't probably be alive for much longer, and God had a message for her."

"That's great honey, I'm glad you were listening to His voice." I paused. "You don't have to say anything. The message was for her to hear and you to deliver."

I stood and moved toward the buffet." Now, I need to go get some food I can eat"!

Our outings were not frequent due to her constant pain and weakness. Des was no longer on a chemotherapy treatment but the bone pain seemed to stay with her. She would refer to it as ghost pains, as sometime it was in her knees, then her hips, her ribs or somewhere else in her body. It was annoying, but not paralyzing.

I had sent an email requesting that our friends call prior to any visits and that when they did come to visit that it would be limited to short time periods. Des would receive phone calls from former clients and continued to share her faith and confidence in God's ability to heal. I remember her telling someone on the phone one day, "I may never be healed physically in my body, but I have experienced so much healing emotionally and spiritually. I can't believe it took me all these years to realize I had to listen to God's voice and that He truly was talking to me."

Each and every phone call ended with a time of prayer with the person. Des told me, "I don't want to miss an opportunity to have the Lord included in my friendships."

"That's a good thing, Des. He is the only one who really counts." I was thrilled to watch her faith increase and her confidence grow during those months. We spent a lot of time reading the Bible together, and in the evenings, we would open a hymnal and sing several songs together. I must admit, I couldn't carry a tune at all, but Des didn't mind. She told me one night, "You know what I love about you"?

"What, that I'm so cute"? I joked back.

"No, but that's true too. What I really love is that you sing from your heart and even if you are off tune, you don't care if anyone hears you, and you're not embarrassed at all. That is so neat." She gave me a hug.

"Well, the Bible says make a joyful noise unto the Lord. It doesn't say it has to be in tune."

In mid August of 2004, Des came to me with a request. "This will be your 60th birthday next month. I'd like to make another trip up to Washington and celebrate it with your twin sister."

"Do you feel up to another trip"? I questioned.

"Well, I thought we could take the car as it is more comfortable to ride in, and the seats go all the way back so I could rest. The truck might be more practical, but I can't climb in and out of the back any longer."

"I suppose that would work. We could always stop along the way if you got tired. We could make it in a couple of days."

Des grinned. "Well, actually, I want to take a longer route. I want to go up 395 and through Eastern Oregon, and up to Glacier National Park, then through southern British Columbia again." She paused. "Then, we could come through the Cascade National Park in Washington and go on down to Aberdeen and celebrate your birthday."

"This is a major trip. Are you sure you're up to spending that many days on the road"?

She came over and put her arms around me. "This might be the last trip we take, and I want it to be special."

"Every trip we take is special," I chuckled. "Let's just make sure we have enough meds for you, and if that's where you want to go, then that's what we will do."

Within a couple days, I had the car serviced and packed, and we were on the road. We stopped in Sacramento to see her son, Phillip. The morning we were leaving, the car seemed to have a missing sound to the engine, but it didn't seem to be serious. We had cell phones and our route would take us through areas that could provide assistance if we had car problems. The second day, we were near the town of Burns Oregon when the car acted as if the transmission were going out. I pulled into a motel for the night, and made a call to a local mechanic. He test drove the car, but couldn't diagnose the problem.

"If you were my mother," he said slowly. "I would recommend you not take this car on the route you've planned. This is the last town for several hundred miles and you don't want to get stuck in the mountains."

I told Des his recommendation. We looked at the map and decided to head west for Bend the next morning. During the night she began to run a high temperature, and her bones were causing her a lot of pain. We discovered we had left her morphine patches at home. I called our next door neighbor and had her go in and Fed-ex them to the motel. I planned to stay one more day until they arrived.

The next morning, her condition had worsened and Des was in a panic. "You need to get me home," It wasn't a suggestion, but a command.

I left our forwarding address with postage so that the clerk could send the patches to us, and we got on the road toward Bend, so I could head south back to California. We were about 80 miles outside of Bend when the car died. I walked to a small café and called AAA. He told me it was lucky where we had stopped, because that was the border to their territory. It would take an hour before the tow truck would be able to reach us. I walked back to the car, sat in the driver seat and burst into tears.

"I'm so sorry Des. We never should have taken this trip." We had our little dog with us too, and the temperature was near 90 degrees. "I can't take any more stress." I looked at Des. She was perspiring and burning up with fever. "I'm going to get you to the nearest airport and fly you home. I'll leave this car in Oregon if I have to." I was sobbing uncontrollably.

"Things will be ok, Darlene. I just need to get some pain meds and rest. We can get the car fixed in Bend." She tried to encourage me.

The tow truck driver arrived and took us to a reliable place of repair just off SR 20 in Bend. It would be the next day, we were told, before they could check it out. The tow truck driver took us to a motel and we settled in for the night. Early the next morning, Des was shaking me awake.

"What's wrong"? I managed to wake up enough to hear her.

"You need to get me to an emergency room. Call a taxi now"! She was struggling to breathe.

I jumped out of bed and called a cab. I dressed as I waited for the taxi, and then got Des dressed. We left our dog in the room as we raced off to St. Charles Medical Center hospital. When we walked through the ER doors, we had no idea that it would be eight days before Des would be coming out of the hospital!

She went through dozens of tests on her heart and lungs, blood work and every test that seemed reasonable. We gave them her cancer history, and each day waited for some news as to what was causing the high fevers, and breathing problems.

I called my sisters and told them we wouldn't be making it up to Washington. The car was repaired by the second day, with reattaching a wire that had shaken loose to the engine. I made daily calls to family and friends, and keep everyone informed as to the tests that were being done, and the results, which all proved negative. I was afraid each time I left the hospital that I would return and be told Des had died. I believed that God was in control our lives, but I was not in control of my fears. My sister Debbie drove down and spent several days with me, and her daughter, Lynda, also drove down to visit with Des. It seemed to make it less emotional having family to share the waiting time.

It was Labor Day weekend, when the doctors decided to release Des. We would return to California and get her checked out by her oncologist.

I prayed all the way home that the car would not experience any further problems, and that I could get Des home with no further problems. We took our time driving, and spend the night in Weed. It was too long a trip to make without stopping overnight. I lay awake watching her sleep, and listing to the erratic breathing patterns. *God, help me to know how to take care of her. Please don't let her die.*

The next morning we rose early and headed for home. We talked openly and honestly about our feelings of fear and that death could come at any time. Des told me on more than one occasion, "You know I'm ready to go Home to be with the Lord. I feel like a car that's running out of gas. I wish I didn't have to leave you and my family." She paused. "I know that when the time comes, it will work out. Darlene, promise me that you won't let them put me in some home or die in the hospital. I want to be home with you."

"I promise" I said. My teeth bit into my lower lip. "No matter what it takes, I will take care of you, and I won't let you suffer or be in pain."

"I'll hold you to that," she said quietly.

Once we arrived home, the next weeks became a blur of doctors' visits, and more tests. I hardly remember my birthday. Des wasn't feeling up to going out, so our friend Becky brought a meal and we had a quiet celebration. Des kept apologizing that she couldn't go out and get me a card. I assured her that it was fine. A card was the last thing on my mind.

Des was scheduled for a brain MRI that next week. The test came back positive for cancer in the lining of the brain.

It was just over three years since that first spot in her lungs. Each new area was still a place where the breast cancer cell had taken hold in her body. They scheduled her for more radiation. Each treatment seemed to be worse than the last. Her head had severe burns, which even the aloe vera didn't help. Mood changes were more obvious. At Thanksgiving, the weekend with her parents was filled with stress. Des didn't feel the radiation was helping, and wanted to stop her treatments. I spoke with the doctor, and we made the decision to stop radiation and go back on chemotherapy. She didn't want visits from anyone but her son, and closest friends. Each day was like a precious capsule of conversations that I thought I would always remember. The words have faded, but the love and devotion have remained strong.

One night we were lying in bed and talking about the day. I asked her how she was feeling. She reached over and took my hand.

"Darlene, I want you to listen to me." Her voice was firm. "I mean it. I want you to hear what I'm saying."

"I'm listening to you, honey." I responded

"There are two things I need you to know. February 14th has always held bad memories for you since that's the time your mother died. I want you to know that I'm going home on Valentines Day so you won't have another date to mess up your memories."

"How can you say what day you will die, Des? No matter what day you go Home, it will mess up my life."

"Listen to me Darlene, and remember what I'm saying. The other thing is that I know you think you will never love anyone again. I've given a lot of thought and prayer to this and there are a lot of women who would be lucky to have you for a mate."

I started to object. "I'm not interested in having another lover, Des. You are the only one I want."

"Listen to me, Darlene." She was almost yelling as she gave me her verbal list. "These women will not be good for you. They will use you and take advantage of you! I know these things." Then she paused. "The only one I can approve is Becky."

"Becky"? I was shocked. "She has been single for a hundred years! Besides, I'm not interested in a new relationship. Not with Becky, not with anyone"!

"You just remember what I said." She paused. "Promise me."

"Ok, Des. I promise you! But you need to know that no one will ever replace you in my heart." We held each other and wept late into the night.

The next morning she sat on the edge of the bed. "I thought of something else I want you to do after I'm gone."

"What's that"? I responded.

"I keep having a vision of an angel carrying me away to Heaven. I want you to have our friend Mike Bennett create a sculpture with an angel and a single breasted woman being held in his arms. I want that to remind you of where I've gone."

"I won't need a sculpture to do that honey. I'll talk with him today and let him know that is your request."

Later that day, I called Mike. He had made a sculpture for us a few years earlier of two women with bald heads, holding one another. It was a one of a kind sculpture, as this one would be also.

He listened to my description. "I will make it for Des and you, Darlene. But not after she passes away. I will get to work on it and have it by Christmas. I want for her to be able to see it since it is her vision."

"Thank you, Mike. I really appreciate it." My voice chocked. "I think we've got a few months yet."

I never shared about Des and my conversations about her going Home in February. I held tightly to the hope that this round of Chemotherapy would knock the cancer into remission.

Christmas 2004 found us spending most of our time at home. Each chemo treatment created a higher risk of infection due to Des' compromised immune system. Phillip and his fiancé Sabrina came over and spent the night along with Des' mother and Father. I knew in my heart that this was our last Christmas together and each day was more stressful than the last. Des and I would talk late into the night, trying to say goodbye, yet not wanting to let go. I became very protective of her time allowing only short visits from anyone other than family.

Mike Bennett came over just before Christmas and brought the most beautiful sculpture I'd ever seen. The angel was kneeling on one knee behind a naked, single breasted woman who was reaching heavenward. The angel had his arms around her waist, and wings on his shoulders. The woman was obviously "going home" and being carried in the arms of God's anointed one.

Des was thrilled when she saw it. "That is exactly what I had in mind," she exclaimed. "Darlene, take a picture of us with the statue. " She reached out and took Mike's hand. "You have a very tender heart and are an excellent artist Mike. You have captured my angel"

Tears were running down his cheeks. "This is one that I wish I didn't have to create."

I picked up the camera and snapped their photo, then picked up my journal and wrote the following poem.

GOING HOME

My angels embrace to guide me home
His strength is replacement for my own
I lift my arms, I'm heaven bound
Listen real close, for the heavenly sound.
Jesus is waiting, He'll wipe away tears
"Just be at Peace," "Release your fears";
Home at last, I'm whole again,
A brand new journey will begin.
Family and loved ones are waiting there,
A new eternity we will share.
God knows the day and the hour
When angels will lift, by their power
And take me home to finally rest
A beloved daughter, not a guest.
To those I leave behind for now,
You will find peace, and then, somehow
You'll sense my presence, for you see;
The woman I am, won't cease to be.
The love we share down deep within,
Will keep us close, it will not end.
Great is Thy faithfulness, it will not fail;
All of His promises, will prevail
In the blink of an eye, I'm finally free
I'll meet you all, in eternity.
Celebrate our lives, and our love,
I'll be watching, from above.

I typed it and placed it in a frame next to the statue. We were living with death, but the end is not yet.

Des and Mike Bennett-Sculptor of an Angel taking woman to Heaven

Statue of single-breasted woman being held by an angel.

Des and Darlene in 1990 taken by Napa River.

Darlene and Des playing in the snow. Taken in Truckee California
1992

Darlene and Des in Hawaii 2000.

This photo was taken of Darlene and Des on a cruise to Alaska. It was taken on one of the formal dinner evenings. It is one of the few times you see us in a dress. Photo was taken about 1994

Photo of Des and Darlene under a cabana on the beach in Mexico

This photo of Des was taken in the park one spring afternoon.

Des with her son Phillip, taken when we were on a cruise
In the Caribbean -2003

Three views of Des at different times in her life. On the right she is about two years old. In the middle, she is in her late 20's and on the left she is relaxing against a rock on the beach. This picture was taken in 2003 when we went on one of our last road trips down the coast.

This is a picture taken at our Holy Union Ceremony in March 2003. Des was quite ill, but we were able to cut the cake and celebrate with friends. On this occasion we wore matching purple dresses. The arch was decorated from the flowers that each of our friends brought to celebrate our special day.

This picture is of the quilt that Becky made for Des on the occasion of her 50th Birthday. Des loved hearts and Becky blended together several heart images. The back of the quilt was also different sized hearts and Becky included the pink ribbon symbol to support Des' battle with breast cancer.

CHAPTER SEVEN
PROMISES MADE-PROMISES KEPT

I am amazed that time can fly by, and drag out at the same time. We made it through the Christmas holidays. It was increasingly difficult to lift Des, or help her stand from a seated position. I received the authorization to have a hospital bed delivered to the house, and we set it up in the front room. Des could look out the front windows, and visitors didn't have to come to our bedroom. It was motorized, so I could raise and lower her easily. I rigged up a buzzer system so that she could ring a bell if she needed me during the night. I placed a walkie talkie by her bed, so that we had contact when I took the dog for a walk. Life was changing on a daily basis. The new pet scan showed aggressive advancement of cancer to her liver, lower lung and lymph nodes. The oncologist suggested we try Gemsar, a new chemotherapy as a last resort.

Des' appetite had decreased and she was on a mostly liquid diet. I had noticed that she appeared more confused as to dates and procedures, and had expressed concern about stopping the chemo for fear of immediate death. I spent a lot of time feeling numb, and crying.

On January 8th, we marked our 12th anniversary of being life partners. On January 12th Des celebrated her 52nd Birthday. I had a friend stay with her while I went to the party store and picked up a helium tank. I filled up 52 balloons and let them loose in the front room. They covered the ceiling above her bed. When she awakened from a nap and opened her eyes, they sparkled with delight. Her mother and dad came up later in the day from southern California to be here for her birthday.

They have been really trying to be supportive. Des has expressed frustration at her mother's inability to retain information, and also that she won't talk about her feelings. We all are aware that these are the last days of Des' time on this earth. Time is running out for her mother to share her feelings and bring healing to their relationship. I am frustrated that I can't make it all happen.

A very scary thing happened one night after her parents left for home. They had spent almost a week with us, and Des was exhausted from all the people that had come to visit. She asked me to not allow so many visits. I would sit quietly in her room, and then go to bed about midnight each evening. I was trusting in the buzzer system I had installed.

One night I was jolted from a deep sleep by a loud thump. I rushed to the front room and found Des on the floor in front of the television. She had been trying to reach the port-a-potty I had placed by her bed.

My heart was racing as I knelt by her side. "Are you hurt"? I was screaming. "Why didn't you call me"? I was checking her body for any cuts or bruises.

"I wanted you to be able to get some sleep," she muttered. "I'm not hurt. Can you get me back on the bed"?

I tried to lift her but was so afraid of doing damage to her bones. "Are you sure you are not hurt"? I asked again.

"I didn't hit anything except the floor. Put a gown on me and call 911. They will come lift me back into the bed." She was calm. We both realized that I couldn't move her by myself, and that this could have been much more serious.

I called 911 and while we waited, I dressed her, and held her in my arms. "Honey, if you break a bone they won't let me keep you at home. Promise me you won't try to get up without my help"!

"I promise." She whispered. "Thank you for making me decent before the firemen arrive."

It was a few minutes later when the truck arrived and I let two firemen into the front room. They checked her for injuries, then lifted her gently back onto her bed. I thanked them then walked over to Des. I was crying as I wrapped my arms around her. "I think your angels were working overtime tonight. It is a miracle that you weren't injured." I glanced at the place she had landed when she fell. There was a narrow space between the recliner and the sharp edges of the television stand.

"I felt like I was being held and lowered to the floor" she said.

"Well it sounded like a truck hit the house"! I laughed out of stress. "Would you tell your angels to be gentler next time"?

"There won't be a next time. I promise not to get up without having you here."

I started sleeping in the recliner in the front room so that I would be able to hear her during the night, and be able to talk with her when she would awaken. I didn't trust her resolve to ask for my help.

The early morning hours became our quality time for talking and praying together. There were no phone call interruptions, and no drop in visitors. Almost every evening she would ask me to read sections of scripture to her. The Psalms seemed to bring a sense of comfort and peace. Although she wasn't up to singing with me, she requested that I go through a hymnal and sing several songs to her every evening. She would reach out and touch my arm as I sat beside her bed.

"You may not be on key, but you sound beautiful to me," she whispered. "I love it when you sing for me."

Eventually, she would doze off and I would return to my recliner. It seemed like the fear of not hearing her when she called, or deeper yet, the fear that she would stop breathing and leave me in the night, kept me awake more often than not. We spoke often of when she would be going home to be with Jesus. She reminded me one night when we were talking and crying together.

"I told you months ago when it would happen." She whispered. She gulped back the sobs that erupted. "I'm going to leave on Valentines' Day." She paused, and then continued. "When the time comes, I only want a memorial service. I want you to officiate and you can do it here at the house if you want. I'd like David to sing, Cathy to sing, and Sherri and the girls to sing my favorite songs." She continued with specific details, and I promised I would do what she requested.

I remembered that conversation from October. It seemed so long ago, and so unlikely that Des would know when the angels would take her to heaven. I was aware of every day and January was drawing to a close. My mind was screaming. *No, you can't go on Valentine Day or any other day. I don't want you to die I don't want to live without you.* I bit my lower lip and sniffed back the tears. I exhaled deeply. "I know, honey. You are going to give my mom a big hug for me and tell her I love her."

"She already knows that Darlene. She loves you too, and is very proud of you." Des spoke with the conviction of someone who had heard those words direct from my mother.

"Well, we haven't given up on this new Chemo yet." I squeezed her hand. I wept freely when we were together, and tried to be accepting and resolved to the eventuality that we were losing this battle. I couldn't bring myself to speak those words.

"I want you to promise me something." She met my gaze, her eyes filled with tears.

"Anything," I whispered quietly.

"I want you to stay close to my parents. I hate it that I won't be here to take care of them. I know my brother Donnie will do what he can, but I always wanted to be there for my folks in their old age."

"I can do that Des. I'll try to be a daughter to them."

"After I'm gone, you can tell them about us. I don't know exactly how they will react, but they love you and I hope they will accept you as a daughter."

"I'll tell them, Des. Actually, what I'll tell them is that you are my very best friend, and I loved you deeply. They already know that."

"Tell them that we were partners. You can tell my brother and Sherri also. I want them to know that our love is real and not something to be kept in a closet! You mean more to me than anyone in the world Darlene, and I want my family to know. I'm sorry I didn't tell them myself." She paused and wiped a tear from her cheek. "I couldn't handle the rejection." Her voice became a whisper.

"It's fine Des. I'll tell the world."

"I want you to promise me that you will write our story. I know there are so many who read your first book and they need to know that God has brought you real love, and blessed our relationship. God will not reject them and He didn't make a mistake in giving them feelings of love for the same sex. You promise me that you will write the truth."

"I promise, Des." My tears streamed down my cheeks. "I don't want you to die. I want you to fight this cancer. We aren't ready to say good-bye."

"I will always love you Darlene, and the love we have will live forever. When it's right, you will love again. Our story isn't finished yet."

I leaned down and embraced her. My tears fell on the pillow, and my heart pounded against my rib cage. "I don't want to ever love anyone again Des. I don't know how I'll live without you."

"You'll never be without me. Just get quiet and listen. You will hear me and feel me with you." She pushed me back so she could see my face. "One more promise."

"What's that"? I asked.

"I want you to stay close to Phillip. I know that Nathan has his own thing, but Phillip loves you and will be there for you if you let him."

"I will try to stay close, Des. I love him and Sabrina, and as long as he wants me to be part of his life, I will be there."

"I want you to go to his wedding in May and be his mother in my place." Her voice was stern. "Promise me."

"I will be at the wedding, and so will you!" I responded. "I may take you in a wheel chair, but we'll be there."

"Just remember what I'm saying to you, Darlene. We don't have that much time."

"I'll remember," I promised. I wasn't sure what tomorrow would bring, let alone four months down the road.

Des had other requests that she wanted the assurance that I would follow when the time came. There were individuals who had proven their friendship over the years and she wanted them remembered in special ways. I made notes of her requests, and promised to fulfill them all in the months after her death.

Our nightly talks continued, as did her chemo treatments each week. I watched for dramatic results, new strength, or less pain. I didn't see anything that encouraged me.

February 3, 2005 was a scheduled doctor appointment and chemo day. Des woke me up about 7 A.M.

"I want to have a shower before I go to the doctor today." She was in her determined mode.

"I don't think I can lift you into the shower, Honey. Can I just bathe you in bed"?

"No, I want a shower"! She reached out to me. "Just get me on the walker seat and roll me to the bathroom."

"I can do that, but the walker won't fit in the shower and there is no place for you to sit down. I don't think this is going to work."

"Please try, Darlene. I feel so cruddy, I just want a shower"! Her arms slipped around my neck and I lifted her to the walker seat. "We can do this. I'll help you," she promised.

Minutes later we were in front of the shower door. It was no use. The strength in her legs was gone, and I had no leverage to place her in the shower. "This would be a cute place for the firemen to rescue you." I tried to joke with her.

"There's got to be a way," she was crying in frustration.

"I've got it." I rolled her walker to the kitchen. "Just sit still, and don't fall." I grabbed a dozen large towels and placed them on the floor in front of the kitchen sink. Then, I rolled her walker as close to the sink as I could manage. I removed her clothing, got a wash cloth and soap and turned on the water. I pulled out the sprayer from the right side of the sink, and got the right temperature. "Shower time," I giggled as I gave her a shower. The towels were soaked when I finished, but Des was happy to be clean.

I dried her, then rolled her back to her bed and got her dressed. "Now, I'll mop the kitchen floor and complete two projects at the same time. I chuckled to myself at my inventiveness for meeting her need and not placing her in danger from falling.

The trip to the doctor's office seemed more difficult. Des was less able to assist me in transferring her from the car to the wheelchair. I had to ask for help from a man in the parking lot.

We went to the office and the nurses took her usual blood sample to make sure the white count was high enough to handle the chemo. Dr. Da Rosa came into the office to talk with us before the treatment.

"Des, I always promised you I would be honest with you. Your white cell count is fine, but the last blood test we did showed your liver numbers to be above 800. I could give you chemo today, but it would do more harm than good. This chemotherapy is not making the impact that we had hoped. It's time to stop the treatments." His voice was kind, but firm. "It's time to go home and rest, Des."

She looked up at me. "But my white cells were fine." She was trying to protest.

"I know honey. What the doctor is saying is that if we give you more treatments that it will not do any good, and it could cause more damage to your liver."

Tears were streaming down her cheeks as the doctor walked from the room. "But you told me you wanted me to fight." She took a deep breath. "I don't want to die."

"I know honey, but now it's time to rest. Your body is worn out and can't fight any longer." I held her for the longest time. "We need to go." I whispered.

I wheeled her to the door and stopped. "I need to go ask the nurses something. I'll be right back."

I stepped into the hall and walked to the nurse's station. "I need to know based upon your experience, how long do we have"? The tears rolled down my cheeks.

They looked at each other and Tina responded. "It could be two weeks, no longer than a month."

Each of the nurses came out and walked over to Des and hugged her. I head one of them whisper, "I'll see you in Heaven Des. Tell Jesus hello from me."

Des seemed in shock as I wheeled her back to the car. "We need to tell Mother and Daddy, and Donnie and Phillip." She seemed to just talking to herself, rather than to me.

"We'll call everyone when we get home, Des." I struggled to get her in the car, and then rolled the wheelchair back to the office. The doctor came over and took my hand. "I'm arranging for hospice to contact you this week." His voice was gentle. "I'm sorry."

"Thanks." I murmured. My eyes filled with tears. "Thank you for being honest with us."

I left the office and returned to the car. Des sat motionless as we drove home. We had talked about this day for almost three years. *God, you promised you would give us the strength for each day Please help us to trust you for this process of letting go.*

The next few days left me numb. I was filled with so much emotion that I couldn't seem to express. I made all the phone calls to family and friends. My sister Debbie and her husband Quin would be coming down at the end of the week. We had an endless stream of friends who wanted to come say a prayer or just sit in silence.

The nights seemed longer for me. I listened to her breathing and it seemed to be more labored as the days passed. Sometimes it seemed that she wasn't breathing at all, and I would panic until I heard her exhale. My thoughts and memories tumbled through the past 12 years and all I could scream silently is *It hasn't been long enough1*

I would take a shower and stand under the water sobbing uncontrollably. *Darlene, you need to be strong for Des.* I told myself. My strength would come in weakness, and the tears seemed endless. *How can I live when she dies? God, I want to die too.*

Des sensed my intense grief and seemed to know just what to say. "Darlene, you don't have to be strong. You don't have to be anything. We have had the years God intended for us to share, and you will go on. You better do the things we would have done together. I know you are hurting, but you know that I am going to be with the Lord. It's not fair, but it is God's will. You promised you would be there for my folks."

"I will be there, Des. I just love you so very much." I put my arms around her. "I miss you so much already."

"I'm not gone yet, so let's cherish the time we have left." She held me close, and we wept together. It was Sunday February 6th. Later that day, Debbie and Quin arrived from Washington to spend a week.

The next few days were filled with phone calls from distant friends who wanted to say good-bye. The Hospice nurse came and filled out dozens of forms. I knew in my heart that it wouldn't matter what information we shared. Des was on a liquid only intake and we had put her on a catheter because she hasn't the strength to stand, even with my help.

She woke me about 4 A.M. calling my name softly. I moved to her side and began to stroke her arm. "What is it honey"?

"I want you to call Becky. Have her bring me some soup. She's the best cook I know."

"I'll do that in the morning. It's way too early to get anyone up. I'll call her first thing."

"This is important Darlene. Tell Becky she needs to come bring me soup." Her tone was insistent.

"I promise I'll call first thing." I knew from our friendship with Becky that she was not an early riser. I hoped that she would make an exception to her no calls before 9 A.M. rule. I sat with Des until she eased back into the labored breathing pattern that told me she was asleep.

The next morning, I called Becky and told her that Des had called for her in the night. I asked her if she could fix some soup and come for a last visit with Des. She promised to be there before noon. I was happy for the visit, and the soup was one meal I didn't have to fix. Des took a couple of sips, but was happy just to have Becky come visit.

I had begun the emotional separation process. I called to cancel Des' charge cards, and remove her name from the paperwork on the truck when I processed the renewal fees. I was trying to have things taken care of by the time she passes. I knew I wouldn't be thinking straight when that happened.

Debbie was a real help. Her years of working in a convalescent hospital were beneficial in this situation. She helped me turn Des every couple of hours so she didn't get pressure sores. She offered to stay with her so that I can get away for short periods and run the errands that needed to be done.

On February 8th, I remembered it was a nephew's birthday, and also our 12 year 1 month anniversary. Des woke me up at 3:30 A.M and asked me to hold her hand. I quoted Scripture to her and sang her favorite songs. I stroked her arms and wiped her down with a wet cloth. I have increased her morphine to every couple of hours. I promised her that I wouldn't let her be in pain, and at this point, I want her comfortable. It makes her sleep most of the time, but she will not die in pain.

We had a funny experience today. I was in the kitchen and Quin came in and sat down.

"I think you need to talk to Des." He had a strange look on his face.

"What's wrong"? I questioned.

"She wants me to move her bed to where the television is, and move the TV to the front window."

"What"? I was surprised.

"Well, that's what she said." He shook his head. "What do I do"?

I walked in and sat down beside her bed. "What's going on Des? You want the bed moved to the side window"?

She looked at me with frustration. "Yes"! she said emphatically.

"Why"?

"Can't you see all those people? They want to come see me. It's brighter over there."

I looked out the window under the carport. I dawned on me that she was seeing people on the other side and needed to have them closer.

"It's alright Des. How about we just leave you where you are and I'll go out and tell them to come see you one by one. They will be able to see you. I'll leave this light on above your head. OK"?

She nodded. She closed her eyes and a smile formed on her lips.

"It's ok, honey. I know who they are." I kissed her forehead.

I walked outside and Quin followed. "Do you think she's having delusions"? He asked.

I smiled. "No, I think she's seeing her grandmother, her Aunt Miriam, and a host of others who are waiting for her on the other side. Mom's probably there too!" I spoke aloud to the unseen images. "Ok everyone, you can go visit with Des one at a time. She's not quite ready to cross over, but if you need to visit her now, go ahead."

Quin looked at me like I was nuts.

"I told her I would tell them, so I did." I walked back in and over to Des' bed. "Ok Des, if any of them need to visit, they will. I told them it was ok, or they could wait for you on the other side."

"Thank you," she whispered and fell asleep.

Her mother and dad arrived later that night. Phillip was coming over on Friday. I called her brother Donnie and his wife and told them that the end was near and they should come as soon as they could. It was February 11th.

On Friday, Phillip and Des' dad were in the front room standing by her bedside. I had gone to the family room, to give them some privacy and was talking with Debbie and Quin. All of a sudden I heard a loud yell from the front room.

"Wahoo"! It was a clear, strong utterance.

I came running. Phillip and Des' Dad were standing on each side of her bed. They had been talking with her for several minutes when she suddenly sat up and let out her favorite war hoop of pleasure! She lay back on the bed, eyes wide open, with a big grin on her face.

Dad turned to me. "I think she just saw something on the other side that made her very happy"!

I looked at her face and eyes. There was no sign of fear. I moved next to her bed and took her hand. "Can you tell us what you are seeing, Des"? She hadn't spoken in over 24 hours, although we continued to talk with her and include her in all the conversations. She closed her eyes and a peaceful smile was all that indicated she was happy with what she had experienced. Those were the last words that she actually uttered. We knew she could hear us, but she never tired to communicate with anyone.

I was still giving her morphine every two hours, and applying the morphine patch to keep her pain level managed.

On Saturday the 11th, Quin had to return to Washington. Debbie promised to stay for another week, to help me. Donnie and Sherri arrived from Southern California. Her oldest son Nathan arrived from Sacramento. Des was aware of his presence, but if he had anticipated a conversation with her, he was too late. I encouraged him to sit by her side and talk with her. They had been estranged for almost three years, and I knew that she would forgive him, even if she couldn't voice the words. The day was filled with tension and emotion as we all carried on quiet conversations in the front room.

Becky arrived mid morning for a last visit. She brought more homemade soup, and a DVD of ocean sounds and scenes. I put it on the television for background ambiance. I told Des that even though we couldn't go to the ocean, that Becky had brought the ocean to her.

It was about noon when I asked Sherri to run to the store with me, so we could fix lunch. On the way, I decided this was the time to address Des and my relationship.

"Sherri," I began. "I know that we haven't spent much time with you and Don. There are some things that Des wants you to know." I paused. "She never felt that she could talk with you or the folks because she was afraid of being rejected. Our relationship is much more than roommates. We are committed life partners and have registered with the state as such. We had our wedding ceremony a couple of years back, and our love for one another is deeply rooted in our faith. We believe that God brought us together, and He has blessed our union."

She was listening intently. "Donnie and I have talked about this, and we already knew that you were a couple. Our church teaching is different than what you believe, however we love Des and we would never reject her. We are not here to judge either of you. Judgment is the responsibility of the Holy Spirit. We will love her always."

Tears were flowing down my cheeks. "I hope you tell her that, Sherri. She has lived in such fear of this ever being talked about in her family. She also told me the other night that I could tell everyone now, and it didn't matter. I haven't voiced the words to her folks, but they can see how much I love her and that my loss is that of not just a best friend, but a spouse."

"We are here to say good-bye and to support you in any way we can, Darlene. Thank you for sharing this with me."

"I decided I needed to do that, because at her funeral there are going to be a lot of gays and lesbians, besides all of our straight friends and family. I wanted you to be aware of our community before the day actually arrives."

We'll handle it just fine." She assured me.

"Also, I would like for you and your daughters, Tammy and Kelli to sing Des' favorite song. She's requested that you sing, 'Great is Thy Faithfulness'."

"We'd love to take part in the service and sing for her. Just let us know when the service will take place." She reached over and patted my arm. "We will be here for her, and for you."

"Thank You," I murmured. "I don't think that I will have this conversation with her dad and mother. There isn't any purpose served in telling them at this point."

The day continued to be filled with visitors and family. The hospice nurse called and gave me instructions on how to handle the last hours, and who to notify when death occurred. It seemed so matter of fact.

Early in the morning of February 13th, I was sitting by Des' side. Everyone had gone to their motel, or to bed in the house. Phillip and his future wife Sabrina were there, and Nathan had decided to stay the night. I told him it would only be a matter of hours and if he wanted those last minutes with his mother, he should stay. Debbie was sleeping in the spare room.

I sat by Des' side, and told her of the day's events. I read to her the notes people were leaving in the guest book. I read several scriptures to her. At one point, I crawled into bed behind her and wrapped my arms around her very gently. I whispered words of love and thanked her for spending her life with me. "I'll see you in heaven honey. Give my mother a big hug for me." It was almost three in the morning, as I lay there listening to her erratic breathing. I stroked her face. "It's ok to go home Des." I whispered softly.

"It's Valentines Day, and you made it. You can let go now." I crossed my fingers as I lied about the date, figuring that across the international date-line, it was already the 14th of February.

I gently moved off the bed and went to Debbie's room and awakened her. "I think it's time. Will you sit with me"?

"Sure". She got up and put on a robe. Together we walked to the front room and listened to the breathing patterns.

"The most difficult thing for me is watching someone I would do anything in the world for, waiting to die. I can't help her with this part of the journey." The tears streamed down my cheeks.

"She doesn't have long," Debbie said softly, taking my hand in hers.

"I know." I paused. "Should I get the boys up to say good-bye"?

Debbie nodded. We stood there and said our own words of parting. I kissed her forehead, her cheeks and her lips. "It's time to go Des. I'll see you in heaven."

I went to where Phillip and Nathan were sleeping and awakened them. "I think it's just a matter of minutes before she's gone. You better come see her now."

They followed me to the front room and each stood by her side. Phillip took her hand and leaned down and kissed her goodbye. A deep sigh escaped her lips.

Debbie and Phillip said at the same time. "She's gone."

I looked at the clock. It was 4 45 A.M. on Sunday morning. "I better call her folks, and have them wake Donnie." Phillip and Nathan slipped outside for a quiet talk, and I made the call to Des' parents. In the moments before the house filled with people, Debbie and I made sure she was presentable, and I covered her with a sheet. I reached down and stroked her arms and kissed her for the last time. I noticed her wedding ring on her left hand, and gently removed it and placed it with mine. We had designed them to fit together when one of us was gone. "I'm so glad you are out of pain." I whispered softly. "Happy Valentine's Day."

I went to the phone and called hospice. They gave me the information I needed, and the mortuary would call me for the pick up arrangements.

It was just after 5 A.M. when everyone arrived to say their last goodbye. We were all standing around talking, sharing remembrances, when Harold walked over to Des. "Hey guys, come look at Des. She's smiling." His voice was filled with astonishment.

"This has happened in the past few minutes."

We all came and stood by her bed. Sure enough, her lips had formed a beautiful smile and were in a closed position. The stress that had filled her facial lines had smoothed to a peaceful look.

"I think she wanted us to know that she's with Jesus"! I reached down and stroked her head. "This part of her journey is finished."

The mortuary called and said they would send someone right over. We waited, and talked about plans for a service. I shared with them Des' desire and said I would plan if for the following Saturday at the clubhouse. "She's already planned it, so all I have to do is get things together."

When Chapel of the Chimes arrived, everyone except Debbie and me stepped outside. They didn't want their last memories to be of her being taken away. The man who first entered the house was very pleasant and professional. He walked over and looked down at Des. "This woman was a Christian, wasn't she"?

"Yes," I responded. "She's home with Jesus now."

He looked at me. "I have done this job more than twenty years and I can count on one had the number of times I've seen a smile on someone's face. Usually that's our job to try and make them smile."

"I think Jesus did your job this time. She's out of pain, and her spirit is rejoicing with the Lord. She left the smile for a reminder. This body was just worn out, and I know she is happy to leave it behind."

We talked for a few more minutes then she was taken away. Although Des was in heaven, my heart felt like it was broken into a million pieces. I had a picture of her walking and leaping and praising God. It would take awhile before I felt anything but great sorrow.

The day was filled with making phone calls, securing the clubhouse and arranging for everyone to help with the service. Quin would fly back down later that week. Debbie would stay and help me do the things that needed to get done before the service. It became evident that the dozen or so people that Des thought might attend her memorial had grown to over a hundred. The clubhouse was the better option for the service.

By day's end, the house was quiet and everyone was gone except for Debbie. We talked for hours, disassembled the hospital bed and put it on the front porch. I sensed Des there with us, and began to wonder if Heaven wasn't a lot closer than I had been taught.

The week passed quickly and on the day of the service, I was overwhelmed with all of the people who came to pay their respects. The service was a representation of our life together just as our commitment ceremony had been. There were gay and lesbian, heterosexual, African American, Hispanic, Baptists, Pentecostal, Catholic, Buddhist, and every other faith discipline. I stood in front of the display of photographs and items we had brought to represent Des' life. I looked over the crowd and twelve years of memories flooded over my mind. There were memories of visits with her family, and my family. I realized how each of these people was entwined with our lives. I also realized that many of them did not know one another. I decided that the service would be a time to change that lack of knowing. I had each person stand and introduce themselves and tell how they knew Des and to share something personal with their relationship. I would interject information when it was too difficult for someone to talk.

Our friend Becky had prepared the luncheon with help from others, and for over two hours we talked, sang and ate. Des' cousin Carolyn brought a framed picture that was taken of our wedding, and she talked about how special it was to have been included in that event. Des had requested I play the song, "I Hope You Dance" for her sons. We ended the service with the group singing "Great is Thy Faithfulness" being led by Sherri, Tammy and Kelli. It seemed to tie all the thoughts and faiths into a unity that represented our faith and our love.

When the service was over, everyone departed for their homes. I promised to stay in touch and to come visit in the following weeks. My twin sister Arlene, stayed for one more day, so that I wouldn't be totally alone. The house seemed incredibly empty and silent that night.

The next month was filled with trips to Washington, Southern California, and Colorado. I visited friends close by, but always came home to a house that was empty of the life I had shared with Des. I had a million memories of our love and didn't want to move or change anything in the house. It seemed there was endless paperwork for notifying all the agencies of her death, and taking care of legal issues. I was glad that we had planned ahead on how we would handle legal and personal matters.

I was kept busy and sometimes frustrated with the process of obtaining legal documents and being able to resolve an account.

One by one, I began to keep my promise to Des about passing on items to people that she wanted to have a special gift. It helped me to know that bits and pieces of her life were being shared around the country.

Inside my heart, I felt like the bits and pieces of our love were irrevocably broken into a million shattered memories.

CHAPTER EIGHT
CRAWLING THROUGH GRIEF

I've always heard that, that you should not make any major changes during the first year after you lose a mate. I didn't **ever** want to make any changes. I spent the first couple of weeks just wandering through the house, touching things that belonged to Des. I could smell her scent in the closets and in her dresser drawers. I cried myself to sleep every night, and would walk up at three or four in the morning and talk to her. She never answered.

Each morning I would take my shower and weep while the water ran down my face. The emptiness of the house wrapped around my soul like a shroud. I have a million memories, some happy, some sad, but all just a tear away.

I kept busy during the daytime hours, visiting friends and finalizing Des' affairs. I had a headstone designed to rest in the place where we will both one day be placed. I picked up Des' ashes, and brought them home. I placed an altar on the table in the front room with her picture and several items of remembrance. At night I would cradle the urn and bathe it with my tears. I wasn't living through grief, I was crawling and life would never be the same.

Des and I had spent the last three years working on loss and grief. We had talked, cried, kept a journal, and cried some more and said good-bye a million times. I thought I was prepared for this time. I was wrong. No matter how many people I spoke with during the day, or had dinner with in the evening, I was alone. People would call and check on me and I always said I was doing fine. I lied.

Rather than explain how shattered my heart was, I lied. I knew that everyone had their own lives to live, and I needed to find a reason to get up every day and face the hours of loneliness. I wanted to die.

Then, I heard Des. Her voice was as clear as if she had been physically standing in front of me.

"Darlene, you promised to be there for my folks and for Phillip. You promised you would go on living and travel. You know where I am, and we will be together again, but you need to work through this process. You are not alone."

Those words rang in my brain over and over. I would figure out how to live again and allow myself to grieve in healthy way. I read books on losing a loved one, but more importantly, I called a former therapist and made an appointment. My friends needed to be friends, not therapists. I could spend time with them and talk about Des, but I decided not to let them know how empty I felt in my heart.

It was about two weeks after Des' death that Becky called one Saturday morning.

"I've heard the wildflowers are in bloom over by Mt. Hamilton…Do you want to get out of the house for awhile and take a ride with me? We could take pictures and let your Chihuahua, Little Bit enjoy being outside for awhile."

"I don't know Becky. I'm not feeling real sociable these days." I didn't want to say I was depressed.

"It will just be a couple of hours Darlene. You need to get out and enjoy the spring scenery."

I immediately heard Des' voice in my head. *I love to be in love in the springtime. Go enjoy the flowers for me.* "Ok Becky, swing by the house. I'll drive."

We went over to Livermore and took the back roads up toward Mt. Hamilton. Des and I had been on that road many times on our trips to Lake Del Valle. We used to rent a motorboat and go fishing at the lake. Today, I was making a new memory to fill the ache of the old memories. Becky proved to be a good listener. I played several CDs that had special music from Des' service. I felt comforted by the music and being able to share the stories behind why we had chosen those songs. Becky listened quietly. We stopped several times to take photos of the wildflowers.

"I'd like to make a quilt from some of these pictures," she said quietly. "Someday I'll take a class that will show me how to do that."

We drove along in silence, my mind wrapped around the songs on the CD by Beth Baker. There was one song with a phrase, "We can be kind, we can take care of one another…" that was playing. Becky spoke softly. "I have something to tell you Darlene. I don't know how you are going to take this, but I need to tell you."

"Ok, what is it"? I questioned.

"About 2 A.M. this morning I woke up and was suddenly wide awake. I felt Des' presence. I said aloud, Des is that you"? She responded immediately. "I want you to take care of Darlene." I lay awake for the longest time, waiting for something more, but that was all she said."

"Oh, I know what she meant." I said. "I don't see well at night and she probably meant that you should drive me to church or if we went out to dinner. She was always concerned about my ability to see." It made perfect sense that Des would have Becky be my driver. She was about the only single friend we had, and Des was comfortable with her. I had forgotten about Des' comments months before, when we had talked about my dating someone new. Right now, dating was not even in my thought processes. Becky was a good friend, and she cared about me. I was a little jealous that Des would speak to someone else and not talk to me. I missed actually hearing her voice, and yet sometimes in the night I could hear her calling me from the front room. I would run to the front of the house, and be met with emptiness. I longed for her to talk to me. I thought about dying so that I could be with her, but I knew that was out of the question.

We continued our drive and took lots of pictures. Becky didn't mention Des waking her again. I thought it was neat, but didn't place any further importance to the encounter.

We attended a couple of church functions over the next couple weeks, and Becky would drive. I was comfortable with our friendship. My loneliness was not as intense when Becky and I spent time together, and I knew that Des would be happy that I wasn't alone all the time.

The end of March I drove to Washington to spend a couple weeks with my sisters. I took our dog Little Bit, and carried Des' urn with me. I had told Des that I would take that trip north, just to put some distance between me and the physical space of our home. I cried all the way to Washington. March 29th was the two year anniversary of our Holy union ceremony. I didn't share those memories with anyone, because that date would only be special for Des and me. I went up to my mother's grave and talked to her that day, hoping that Des would want to talk to me. *I guess I haven't learned to be quiet enough to listen. Des always said I would have to be real quiet and I would hear her talking to me.* The next day, March 30th was Debbie's 48th Birthday. We got together with Arlene and Charlie and all went out to dinner. I felt like a 5th wheel. This was my first visit in 12 years that Des wasn't with me, and I ached to have her celebrating with us. I cried so much during those two weeks, that I wondered when the tears would stop. I was sure that everyone around me was uncomfortable; however I had no control over the emotions that erupted at a moments notice. I was glad when the visit was over, and I headed back to California. I drove straight through, and made it in 14 hours. I planned to be home for two days, then go to Southern

California and see Des' family. I had some personal items to pass on to them, along with some photos she wanted me to return.

When I arrived in Hayward, I called Becky to see if she wanted to meet for dinner. We went to the Outback Restaurant in Fremont. I shared the events of the past two weeks with her, unable to make it through the meal without more tears spilling down my cheeks.

She listened quietly, and then spoke. "Darlene. What do you need from me"?

Her question took me by surprise. My answer took her by surprise. "A hug." I muttered. "Just a hug."

"I can do that." She moved from her side of the table and stood beside me. I stood and let her embrace me, the tears once again flowing unchecked.

The next day, I met with my therapist. I was concerned that I was losing my mind because of all the tears. Susan told me that I was going to be fine and that my way of grieving was just that, my way. There is no set time frame for the tears to stop. She was glad that I had friends who could share my sorrow and not try to fix me. She also told me that one year to grieve was not a benchmark. Des and I had been on this process for sometime, but her loss would always be present with me. She assured me that it would get better as the months went by, but not to rush the process.

I remember telling her, "I know why Des wanted to die first. I don't think she would have been able to handle this pain. She was good with physical pain, but awful with emotional pain."

"I think you knew her well, Darlene," Susan responded. "You will be just fine."

I made an appointment for two weeks, after my visit to Des' family. I felt better knowing that I had an emotional safety net.

I went home and finished packing the car. I had things to take to Des' family. Des wanted her niece Kelli to have the paintings from her grandmother, her brother Donnie to have the childhood bear, her niece Tammy to have some candles and holders, and her sister in law Sherri to have the piano musical figurine. I brought Harold and Dorothy photos and her Lazy Boy recliner. Dad was turning 79, and I wanted to share in his birthday celebration. I also brought them a copy of a tape that Des had made for them a little over a year ago. She knew she was dying and had left special messages for many of her loved ones. I brought the separate tapes for Donnie and Sherri as well as her folks.

It seemed so strange to be at their home without Des. I lay in the same bed that we used to share, but I couldn't fall asleep. There was still a big hole in my heart.

It seemed good to let Harold just do all the driving and keep active as we visited friends. Harold's driving scares me sometimes and I prayed that God's angels were protecting all of us! We talked of taking a trip to Washington State in May, after Phillips wedding. They wanted to go check on the land in Eastern Washington. They want to sell it back to the Indians. They wanted me to go along to help with negotiations and to help with the driving. I marked my calendar and knew that I would be back from my trip to Denver. I was going to see my niece. I planned on keeping myself busy and hoped that some of the pain would have lessoned by then.

On my way back to Hayward, I drove by Long Beach to see my friend Judy. She had been such a support through the time with Des. She had come up for weekend visits several times during the last month of Des' life. I was comfortable sharing memories and tears with her. We talked of how incredible Des' attitude was about death. She spoke openly of being scared, yet so confident that God was present in every aspect of her journey. Des didn't want to have pain, and she didn't want her life extended by artificial means. Judy was so impressed that I had been able to honor those requests and keep her comfortable, allowing her to spend those last days with the dignity she deserved. I've been told that this was unusual, because many people are not able to handle the stress of watching and waiting for their loved one to cross over. I felt blessed that God gave me the strength to do that, and was aware once again that you never know how strong you are until you are in the situation. I didn't know how long it will take to put the pieces of my soul together, but each friend I visited seemed to add to my healing.

I was home just long enough to unpack the car and repack my suitcase. I had decided to take the train to Denver. Des and I had always talked of doing that, and it would give me a break from driving.

As the scenery passed by, I remembered some of the trips we had taken in past years. My heart aches with the memories. We had many good years together, just not enough of them.

I had received a call from Kathy Mercer, Des' case worker earlier in the week. She asked me if I had gotten angry yet. I paused before I responded.

"I don't feel angry. I feel incredibly sad that she's not here. I'm sad that she was so young and that she lived with so much pain. I'm sad that she spent 5 weeks taking radiation on her brain when it didn't make any difference in the outcome. I'm just sad." I paused, and then continued. "I guess I'm most sad in that however many sunsets or sunrises I have left in my life, she won't be here to hold my hand. Perhaps I'm angry and just don't know how to define it. I don't know who to be angry with, certainly not God. I can't be angry at Des for leaving because I know it wasn't her choice. If anything, I'm angry at Cancer. Mostly, I'm just sad."

I reran that conversation over and over as the miles rolled by. I cradled the urn in my lap as I curled up in the sleeper car. I whispered, *"Thank you for sharing your life with me even though you were in so much pain. I wouldn't have missed the dance for the world."*

I arrived safely in Denver and my niece Angel met me at the station. We had a wonderful week together, and shared a lot of memories about Des. I spent one day at the State Park where Angel works, and saw a red fox and a black bear. Being in nature was a good diversion from the memories and missing Des. It's hard to believe it's only been a month since her death. I brought the video of the service, and shared it with Angel and her husband Jim.

I had a weird dream type vision during the night. I wasn't quite asleep, and not really awake. I had been crying. I saw Des sitting on a bench in a train station. It was very sunny and I saw that she was holding her sun glasses. She also had all of her hair. I watched the scene as my mother came up and sat beside her on the bench. I asked her why she was waiting there. She looked at me and said, "We're waiting for you"

I kept trying to get to where they were, but couldn't find a way to be with them. I kept trying to tell her all the stuff that was happening and asking her how to handle the situations. She looked sad, but just smiled at me. My mom didn't seem to notice I was talking with Des, and then the vision ended.

I knew that my life would never be the same. I kept asking God to show me how to embrace the changes and go on with life. Some days I had to struggle to even want to live another day without Des, but I knew she wanted me to live until it was God's time to take me home. I made a decision to live one day at a time, tears and all.

The train trip home was without incident. I stayed in the sleeper car and wrote in my journal. I've been gone so much I feel like I'm detaching from the house and some of the painful memories. It's difficult because the happy memories are entwined in the painful ones.

I arrived home and stayed one night, then packed up the truck to drive it to Washington to sell to Arlene and Charlie. I only need one vehicle and will keep the new Kia that Des and I just purchased in September.

I spent two days with Debbie and Quin and we talked about taking a trip to Hawaii in October after their fiscal year ended for their uniform business. I gave them $2000.00 from the sale of the truck so that they would have the trip paid in advance.

Debbie asked me if there was someone who might travel with me as a companion, so I wouldn't be alone. "I only have one friend who is single. I don't know if she would want to go to Hawaii or not. I'll call Becky and see what she thinks. You met her at Des' service, so she's not a total stranger."

I called and presented the idea to Becky. She commented that she didn't know if she could afford it, but would pray about it. She said she was fine with traveling with me and my family. I put the trip on my mental agenda, and pretty much forgot about it. This was only the first of May. I left the truck with Arlene, and Quin drove me to Seattle to fly back to California.

My friend Mary, who had been taking care of Little Bit, came and picked me up at the airport. The next two weeks were busy with short trips to visit friends, attend church in San Jose and visit neighbors. I left when I woke up in the morning, and came home late at night. It had been three months since Des passed away.

Harold and Dorothy drove up from Southern California and picked me up for the trip to Lodi. Phillip and Sabrina were getting married, and we were involved in the wedding. I was the Mom #2, and as such, was given a seat of honor at the ceremony. Phillip laid a red rose in the empty seat next to me. I kept talking to Des in my head, trying to not break into tears.

It helped that I got angry with the Des' side of the family. Harold and Dorothy and I were ignored by all the relatives, and treated rudely by the couple of people who did talk with us. I told John that I was disappointed that people who call themselves Christians would treat us with such disrespect. All of them knew about Des and my relationship and that she had recently passed away. Not one of them expressed condolences to Harold and Dorothy, or to me. It occurred to me that I was in the strange situation of being a lesbian widow. I'd never heard of a support group for my category, and no one at the wedding would ever acknowledge our union. I was glad when the wedding was over.

I called Becky to tell her how the wedding had gone, and how angry I was about our treatment. She listened, and then responded simply. "You made Des proud. You were there for her, and I know she was there too."

It helped dissolve the anger.

The next morning, Harold, Dorothy and I headed for Eastern Washington. I alternated driving with Harold to give him a break. We went up Hwy 97, which was the same route that Des and I had taken on our last trip. We got to Bend, where she spent eight days in the hospital. I don't talk about the memories in my head, but occasionally I'd mention that Des and I had been here too.

It would always elicit a comment from Des' mother. "You were such good friends. I know you miss her a lot."

"Yes, I do," I responded. "It helps to know exactly where she is, and that she is with us on this trip."

Her mother looked surprised. "Do you sense her with us too? I feel like she is right with us most of the time."

"Yes, I'm sure she is here," I responded. *You can speak up any time, Des.* My thoughts were never far from engaging in a mental conversation with her.

We arrived safely at the property in Eastern Washington. The next morning, we spoke with the Indian counsel and told them of our desire to sell the land. They put us on a list for the following year, when they might have funds to acquire new land. Our business was concluded and we headed toward Seattle to see Harold's cousin. Our pathway took us through the Cascade National Park. This was part of the scenery that Des had wanted to enjoy on the trip we were unable to finish last August. I snapped lots of pictures and tried to enjoy it for both of us.

Each night when we stopped at a motel, I would take a walk and call Becky. She seemed to be a place of comfort for me, and I shared my feelings about the trip. I felt less alone and connected to someone who also loved Des. In many ways, she was a lifeline to my sense of sanity, and she was so easy to talk with about my grief. I thought God had gifted me with a special friendship.

We spent the night with Harold's cousin, Audrey, and then headed down to Aberdeen to see my sisters again. I laughed when I walked into my sister's office. Her boss greeted me and said "Did you get lost? You were just here."

"Yeah," I said. "I keep trying to get out of this town but the road just keeps bringing me back. Maybe it's an omen!"

I hugged Arlene and made arrangements to have dinner with her and that night Debbie and Quin joined us at the Mexican restaurant. Des' mother's forgetfulness was much more pronounced as I spent longer periods of time with her. She didn't remember meeting my family, and seemed to have no idea which state we were in at any given time. She thought we still had to go see about the property in Eastern Washington, and kept asking if I had ever been in this town. I told her it was where I grew up.

.

It makes me sad that Harold has to deal with this all the time. He has had a lot of years of caring for Dorothy. They have been married almost sixty years. I pray that if anything happens to them, that she will be the one to go first. Dorothy could not live independently if anything happened to Harold.

We left the next morning and headed down the coast for the long trip home. Harold wanted to go by the ocean. He mentioned more than once how much Des loved the ocean. I shared with them the number of times that Des and I had driven on that very road, and how special some of the places were to us. Dorothy was confused as to where we were, where we had been, and when we would arrive at home. I tried not to be impatient with her. A thought occurred to me. *Des, I'm glad that you got to go to heaven before you ended up with no mind at all.*

We took two days to travel the coast, and then Harold and Dorothy dropped me off at home. They got a motel for the night, and left for southern California the next morning. It was Sunday, so I drove to Los Gatos and picked up Becky. We went to church, then out to lunch. I shared the highlights of the trip, I was happy to be talking with someone who would remember ten minutes later what I had just shared.

I spent the afternoon in her living room, rambling on about my feelings of friendship and relationships. I didn't feel ashamed to cry in front of Becky, and noticed that she sometimes had tears in her eyes when we talked about Des.

I wish I could ask her to just hold me, but that might be more than Becky would be comfortable with, or more than I could handle. I feel so isolated from touch. Not the sexual stuff, just the emotional connection of holding hands and talking. Des and I had talked so much about her death and when she would go to heaven, but I never moved beyond that event to imagine what each day would be like without her in it. I had no concept of what day after day without her, would feel like in the depths of my soul. I shared with Becky the loneliness and isolation I feel even when I'm with other people.

She just lets me talk. It's a good thing to have a place of safety.

The next week was filled with a visit to an elderly woman that has me do things to help her, and then trying to clean up the yard at my house. I went to lunch with Cherie and Becky and we spent the afternoon at Cherie's place. Sandy had to work late, so we left mid-afternoon. Becky was going to drive back to Los Gatos. As we walked to the car, she asked. "Are you doing alright"?

"Not really," I responded. "I just don't want to go home alone."

"I'll come for awhile," she responded. "I don't have to go home yet."

She came over and we just sat in my front room. I talked about Des, and cried. I think its so healing that she lets me cry and doesn't try to fix me. It was early evening when she left, and I gave her a long hug before she walked out the door. "Maybe I'll just keep you here and not let you leave," I joked.

We laughed, but I felt a lot of comfort in her hug.

I shared all of this with my therapist on my next visit. Susan assured me that I was progressing through the grief process in a very normal way. She also told me once more that I would be just fine, and how healthy it was to be able to cry and not be stoic and have it all together.

I looked forward to my sessions with her, and somehow I knew that God was bringing healing into my brokenness.

I had a strange phone call about this time. A friend from Chicago called. She had once lived in the Bay Area and knew Des and me from church. After a couple of minutes, she said, "I want to share something with you, but I don't know how you'll take it."

"Not much can surprise me Delores. What do you want to tell me"?

"Does Des visit you"? She asked hesitantly.

"Not as much as I'd like" I chuckled. "Why"?

"I was sitting here last night eating a piece of watermelon."

"She loved watermelon," I interrupted.

"Well, I had finished the watermelon and the rind was in the bowl with my spoon. I had set it on the table in front of me. Suddenly the spoon moved in the bowl and I felt Des' presence."

"That doesn't surprise me Delores. She was very fond of you and appreciated the prayers and the prayer cloths that you had sent to her over the past few months. She probably stopped by to say thanks."

"That isn't all that happened," Delores continued. "I said, "Des is that you"? the spoon moved again. "I was a little unnerved and said 'God Bless you Des'. You can go on your way now." The spoon moved a third time, and I felt like she said good-bye and left.

"That doesn't surprise me at all. She has made a few appearances by the strong awareness of her presence. She spoke to me a couple of times, and she spoke to Becky once."

"That's the really interesting thing. I felt like she wanted me to tell you that it was ok for you to develop a relationship with Becky and that she was supposed to be a very close friend." Delores paused. "I know that sounds weird. Have you spent any time with Becky"?

"I've gone to dinner with her a couple of times and we've gone to church together. I know that Des told me months ago she wanted me to be closer friends with Becky after she was gone."

"Well, I'm just passing on my impressions from this encounter. It is really weird to me. I don't know what I think about talking with dead people."

"The way I look at it, is that she isn't dead. Her body is dead, but the woman she is, still lives in everyone she loved. She's with the Lord, and if He can speak to us from time to time I don't see why Des can't communicate in the same way."

"I told her not to come back, so I don't think I'll be hearing from her again." Delores was serious. "I'm not sure it's Biblical."

"The more I learn about God, and death, the more I'm convinced that we have tried to isolate Heaven as being someplace a million miles away. I don't think it's far at all, and I know that people have come back after their death, all throughout the Scriptures. She can talk to me anytime she wants! I don't think it's something to be afraid of as being evil. Love is eternal, and so are we."

I hung up the phone and spoke aloud. "Well Des, you're just having a ball traveling to all these places aren't you? When are you going to talk to **me** again"?

I sat quietly, but only silence pounded in my head. Once again, the tears streamed down my cheeks.

I was grateful that I had Little Bit to not only keep me company, but keep me active. I had to walk him every few hours. I had a friend, Marsha, who lived just around the corner and she also had a little dog. We would often walk them together, and talk about Des.

She came to the door and knocked. "Hi. Want to go once around the park"?

"Sure." I grabbed Little Bits leash. "Come on kiddo. Let's go for a walk."

"How are you doing"? Marsha asked. "I know you are gone quite a bit."

"It's really hard to be here," I told her honestly. "I miss Des all the time and I know that I won't cry forever, but it seems to be where I am in the process for now."

"Do you think you will ever start dating again"? She asked.

"It's hard to say. I spend a lot of time with friends, but I don't think I will be ready to fall in love for quite a while, if ever."

"I wasn't going to tell you, but several months ago our mutual friends down the street were talking to me and made a comment that they thought you would be with someone before a year had passed."

"What"? I was really shocked.

"It was before Des had even died. They just felt you were the type of person who needed to have someone in your life."

"That may be true, but I'm really upset that they would make that comment to someone else before Des was even dead. That's pretty insensitive."

"I just thought it was inappropriate. I hope that you do find someone to share your life with in the future, but I know how much you loved Des and I don't see that happening for awhile."

"You'll be one of the first to know if it does," I joked. "It will have to be a very understanding woman to live with me with Des' ashes in the front room"!

"Be sure to tell her that on your first date," she joked in return.

Marsha was comfortable to talk with, but not at all my "type" I was glad that she had told me about the comments. I would be more cautious in sharing my feelings with anyone in the future.

I looked forward to my weekly sessions with my therapist. I continued to read books on grieving and to write in my journal. I continued to spend as little time at home as I could, trying to avoid the pain.

On May 9th, Cherie and Sandy and I took Becky to Santa Cruz to celebrate her birthday. I gave her a card with the money to pay for the Hawaii trip. "Consider it a gift from Des and me," I said. "I know she would want you to enjoy one of her favorite places."

Becky was overwhelmed with the gift. I was happy to have a traveling companion that could share some special memories. I didn't want to just be there with Debbie and Quin.

My journey of grief and healing seemed to be on a fast track. I realized I wasn't crying all the time now, and I could talk about Des beyond her last few months. I was able to make some special gifts to the other friends as Des had requested, and in sharing her generosity, I developed an on going remembrance for her.

It occurred to me one evening as I was wandering through the house, touching, smelling and remembering our life together, that I wasn't flat on the floor or crawling any longer. I was walking and looking forward to what life would bring in the days ahead.

This is the first photo taken of Darlene and Becky as a couple.
It was taken in my back yard in 2005.

Photo of Darlene and Becky was taken in Hawaii alongside our condo in Princeville. The garden and the pond in the background captured the essence of the garden Isle-Kauai. October 2005

CHAPTER NINE
NEW MINISTRY-NEW LOVE

The weeks passed, and I continued to reach out to friends, sharing with them Des' vision to reach out to the Gay community. I spoke at a couple of churches and encouraged the congregations to be active in speaking out for God's unconditional acceptance for all His children. If we can embrace the reality that God truly is for us, then it won't matter who is against us.

I had engaged in many long talks with Des about speaking out as Christian lesbians, and letting others know that you didn't have to choose one or the other. Her deep fears of rejection from her family had held her back for many years. I longed to bridge that gap of misunderstanding and share God's truth as we had lived it for more than a dozen years. I prayed that God would provide opportunity and support for this ministry call that was so strongly imbedded in my heart.

One opportunity presented itself when a pastor friend, Elaine Sundby called to ask my assistance on a book that she was writing. She had been the founding pastor of Faith Full Gospel Fellowship, where Des and I had attended until her illness. Elaine was putting the final touches on her book, Calling the Rainbow Nation Home. (Published by iUniverse) She knew that I had authored several books and wondered if I would offer some editorial suggestions on her manuscript. I agreed and read with interest how her journey for truth and acceptance paralleled my own. She went into great depth in reviewing the Biblical Passages that were used to condemn homosexuals, and in the end concluded that homosexual orientation is a gift from God, to be embraced and celebrated. My spiritual journey with Des for more than a dozen years had made the same discovery. I was pleased to share in finalizing her manuscript for publication.

Elaine hosts the website, www.gaychurch.org, which features one of the largest gay Christian bulletin boards and gay "welcoming" Church directories in the world. A large section of the site is dedicated to articles pertinent to reconciling ones faith with their sexual orientation. I hoped that Elaine's book as well as the website would help me to speak more effectively to those in the Gay community who were no longer interested in organized religion due to the rejection they had experienced at the hands of those ministers who claimed to speak for God.

Becky and I prayed that God would help us to reach out to her group of woman that she had dinner with each Wednesday. Many of them professed no faith at all, while others have been so wounded by those who claim to speak for God, that they want nothing to do with any organized religion. We agreed to pray for them and to live out our faith without apology. I joined her on Wednesday evenings for that dinner hour, and started to learn who they were. I was amazed at the hurt and rejection so many had experienced, and decided that it wasn't words I would say but how I lived that might influence them to see a loving God.

Becky and I also decided to actually go out on a date. We went to the movies and saw the new Star Wars film. After the movie, we went to dinner at the Outback. I learned that she had been single for seventeen years and wasn't interested in a lover relationship unless it was with a Christian woman. She had decided that she would rather be single than to pursue a relationship without a faith base, better alone than with the 'wrong' person. That information was a great encouragement to me.

She met my gaze across the table. "Darlene, I really like you. I've watched you care for Des for the past few years, and I know that you need time to grieve your loss. I don't want us to jump into something before either of us can handle it."

"I'm really comfortable with you Becky. I love spending time with you and I've never met a more compassionate person. I don't know what I'm feeling most of the time. I know that I loved Des with all my heart and that I don't have the words to express how much I miss her. I'm asking God to enlarge my heart to make room for a new friend and relationship." I paused. "I know we're not ready for any commitment, but I am open to seeing where God will lead us. I promise to keep on the healing path, and will be honest with you about my feelings."

Her response was thoughtful. "I think we should just see each other, and not make it known that we are dating. We don't need any additional pressure."

"That sounds good to me." I slipped out of the booth. "Let's walk through the mall."

We walked across the plaza and I slipped my arm through hers. "We can just be a couple of old ladies leaning on one another." I smiled and nudged closer. *This feels really comfortable.*

We walked through the mall, then out to our cars. "I'll see you tomorrow." I promised.

"I need to paint the railing on my deck." she said. "Maybe we can do it together."

"I'll bring my old clothes and help you. I'm a good painter!" I declared. "Have a good evening." I walked to my car and drove home. My mind was spinning with trying to deal with this new awakening. *I know Des is approving of this relationship, so I'm not betraying her or our relationship. She encouraged me to reach out to Becky. Is this too soon? How do I start dating again? Des, I miss you so much. I know you don't want me to be alone. I don't know if I can ever love someone again. Dating doesn't' mean I'm in love with someone, it only means I'm open to moving on. I don't want to move on. I want you to be here Des, but you're not, and now I don't know what to do.* My thoughts tumbled through the tears that erupted without warning. I missed Des so much. *Will it be fair to another person to date them when I can't get Des out of my brain or my heart?*

I lay awake for several hours that night trying to have it make sense. The only thought that came to me was "Take it one step, one day at a time."

The next morning I packed my car with painting supplies, and a change of clothes. I drove the 35 miles to Los Gatos and pulled up into Becky's driveway. My heart was pounding against my chest *I've got to know if this is supposed to go any further.*

I got out of the car and walked into her house. "Good morning, Becky." My greeting was cheerful. "Where are you"?

"I'm in the kitchen," she responded.

I walked in and found her at the sink, doing her dishes. "Hey, I have a question. How tall are you anyway"?

She looked puzzled. "I'm Five foot eight. Why"?

I grinned. "I just wanted to know how much you had to bend in order for me to kiss you."

I slipped my arms around her neck and gently pulled her head down to meet my lips. I gave her a quick kiss, and then pulled away. "Ok, that's over. Now I can go paint."

I left a very surprised woman standing in the kitchen.

Through out the day, we talked about where our relationship might go from here. "The only thing I know for sure is that it can't go back to before I kissed you." My smile was a bit mischievous. "We are both committed to serving the Lord, and having our relationship bring honor to Him. I know that God will lead us and I think we should just make sure we continue to pray together and take it one day at a time."

Becky looked thoughtful. "Darlene, I don't want to take Des out of your life, or separate her from our relationship. Your love for her is part of who you are. We'll figure this out in time. I want you to talk to your therapist and if she thinks we should back off for awhile, then I'm willing to do that in order for you to continue your healing."

"I see her tomorrow and I'll talk with her about our steps toward building a relationship." I gave her a long hug. "I think that she will be fine with our process."

I did bring up the topic during my therapy session. Susan's response was immediate. "I think it's wonderful. Your love for Des will always be part of who you are, and she wanted for you to move on with your life. There is no prescribed time table for healing and you and Des worked on the grieving process for a couple of years before she died. You aren't 20 years old, and you don't have years to wait for a socially acceptable time of approval. If you feel God is directing you to move forward, then go for it. You are 60 years old, and I think you and Becky should enjoy your senior years together. If people have a problem with that, then remember that it is their problem, not yours."

I was thrilled that she was encouraging and affirming of this budding relationship. I shared her words with Becky, and we agreed that we were on the right pathway. We also agreed that it would be at least a year before we would consider moving in together. That would give us both time to grow into our union, and get to know one another before we actually lived together.

In the following weeks, it seemed strange to be embracing a new love while learning to release the still fresh memories of Des and our journey. I kept remembering those last days of her life on earth and how I did all I could to make her comfortable, but the one thing I really wanted to do, I was unable to accomplish. That was to keep her alive and cancer free. The memories bring tears, however I feel that I am not as emotionally fragile as I was just three months ago. Each day brings new insights as these two journeys move in unison.

Becky and I have started to teach a women's Bible Study on Thursday evenings. We have opened her home to women of our church and other lesbian women. We've chosen a book titled "Bad Girls of the Bible" by Liz Higgs. It is a challenge to take a look at women from the Bible and relate our lives to theirs. I am encouraged to be reminded that none of us have it all together, without the grace of God.

I received a telephone call this week from a documentary film producer in Santa Cruz. She and her partner are doing a film called, "God and Gays, Bridging the Gap"

They were given my name by Elaine Sundby after they made contact with her on her website. They want to interview me because of my former connection to Exodus International. They are interested in the process of my Exodus from Exodus and how I came to resolve the ex-gay teaching with a full acceptance of God's love for His gay and lesbian children.

I am thrilled to have a part in a project that will speak hope to those who have been rejected and condemned by the mainline Christian community in the name of God. I also feel that this is the first step in speaking the truth and impacting those lives that have been broken by the ex-gay message of "It's a choice and just pray your way to healing".

The film producers have interviewed several people, including Mel White executive director of Soul Force. They tried to get a response from the Exodus International leadership, but were turned down. They were also prevented from attending an Exodus conference and seeking interviews.

I am bothered by the fact that Exodus believes they are standing for God's truth yet they refuse to be part of Bridging the Gap of misunderstanding. I realize now how much damage was done by my former ex-gay ministry and all of the ex-gay teaching. I sincerely wanted to help people who were struggling with their sexual orientation, however I had refused to consider that sexual orientation is a gift from God, and not something that needs to be forgiven or changed. This film is an opportunity for me to step forward and be one small voice for our community. I believe it is the first of many doors that will open on the journey of reconciliation.

The film was released in early 2006 at the Cinequest Film Festival in San Jose. There will be many opportunities for promotion and speaking out to the Gay community as well as the mainline Christian Churches. Becky and I have committed ourselves to supporting the film and being available to speak on behalf of the full acceptance of all God's children regardless of sexual orientation.

Shortly after that interview, another opportunity to take a public stand for being Christian and Gay was presented to us. We attended the Evangelicals Concerned conference at San Francisco State University. Evangelicals Concerned is a similar type of group like Exodus but unlike Exodus, they embrace God's unconditional love and acceptance of the Gay community. They have been in existence about the same length of time as Exodus. Dr. Ralph Blair is the founder of this group, which has grown to have an international impact for the Gay community. I have been on their mailing list for several years, but never attended any of the conferences. One of my fears back in the early 90's was that someone from the group would see Des and me at a function and I would be "outed" in their newsletter due to my former affiliation with Exodus International.

It was really strange to attend the annual conference in San Francisco. The first Exodus conference I ever attended was also at San Francisco State University back in the middle 80's. This conference was a time to share my story and publicly embrace my role as a Christian Lesbian woman. It felt good to have Becky by my side as a supportive partner on this journey.

I was amazed at how many people knew who I was from having read my previous books. I also ran into Mark, the man who used to be the men's leader at my ex-gay ministry a decade earlier. Mark and his partner are active in the Evangelical Concerned Ministry and he has also come to the place of embracing his homosexual orientation as a gift from God. Our encounter brought back a lot of emotional conflicts from the events of being ousted by Exodus from ministry when Des and I became a couple. Once again, it was a unique opportunity to walk in forgiveness of past hurts.

I listened to many stories that weekend of how the church and groups like Exodus had wounded families. I was humbled to realize that God had brought me full circle and now provided me the opportunity to ask forgiveness of some of those family members. I may not have spoken with these specific individuals, but over the years I had counseled many families who had asked for hope. I had told them to pray for their kids and accept them, but not the sin. I wondered how many lives I had shattered with my piety.

I made some contacts with individuals that have web newsletters for the gay community, and feel that God is calling me to once again write His message. I accepted the call once again to write a book to chronicle the journey of understanding and acceptance for not only Des and myself, but for all who make up the Gay community around the world. *This book is one step in fulfilling that call.*

My journey with Becky was forging a new path, no longer paralleling a journey with grief. We are making our own life that is totally separate from the union that Des and I had shared. I will always love and miss Des and I know that our loving commitment is part of what makes me the woman that Becky is falling in love with each day. I am also growing to love and appreciate Becky more with each passing day.

We spent almost every day together, during those first few months, and talked late into the night time hours. We are committed to each other, and when the time is right, we will move in together. Our trip to

Hawaii with my sister and brother in law was coming up in just over a month. Becky had planned a trip to Solvang to celebrate my 61st Birthday in September. Our life together was making memories of our own.

Late July, 2005, brought with it a new sense of permanence. Becky and I went to southern California to visit Des' parents. They have invited us to stay for a few days, and make plans for a cruise in April for Dad's 80th Birthday.

Becky said it felt weird to be in the house where Des grew up, and to be sleeping in the room where she spent her childhood. It was like "being in the twilight zone" to her way of thinking.

I asked, "Do you want to stay in a motel"?

"No." she responded. "It just feels weird."

"Des and I went a lot of places and you and I will be in some of those same places as we travel together. Is that going to be a problem for you emotionally"? I was concerned.

"I don't think so," she replied. "We are making our own memories."

I was happy Becky felt that way, although I knew that there might be some difficult times ahead for us. I kept remembering. *One day at a time.*

When we left Harold and Dorothy's home, we drove to the coast to see our friend Judy. Just before arriving in Long Beach we stopped in Laguna Beach to visit a jewelry store we had found on the internet. They carried a nice selection of rainbow rings. We planned on having a private commitment ceremony on the beach in Kauai when we went in October.

We picked out a matching, yellow gold set of rings with a thin band of rainbow colored stones across the top. The stones were recessed so that they will not catch on material or be likely to cut into our fingers. We agreed to keep them in their boxes until our ceremony in October.

We had a good visit with Judy and made plans for them to join us in Solvang for my birthday. We continued our journey back to San Jose, and decided to stop along the coast when we got to Pismo Beach. It is comfortable to be traveling together and continue to make new memories. Becky is introducing me to her friends along the way, and our lives are blending like the fabric of a quilt.

The weeks passed quickly and I could hardly believe I was turning 61. I was so involved with Des and her illness last year that I didn't even remember celebrating my birthday. I told Becky that I was turning 60 for the second time! She surprised me by having several of the women from our Wednesday night dinner group drive down and celebrate with us. Once again, I see a blending of our separate lives into a new tapestry.

Three weeks later, we arrived in Kauai and met Debbie and Quin at the airport. We had a huge condo on the north side of the island in Princeville. I received a phone message from Judy, and she had flown to the island with some of her friends. Their last night on the Island was our first night. We made arrangements to meet them on Hanalei Beach. It was good to have friends to share or commitment ceremony. My family and Judy took pictures and made a video of us sharing our vows on the beach. In the middle of a rain downpour, we began our life together as a couple, witnessed by family and special friends. Most importantly, our vows were witnessed and blessed by our Lord and Savior, Jesus Christ.

New love, new life, new ministry combined with new challenges that day on Hanalei Bay. Our rainbow rings hold the promise of growth together in our senior years. There have been concerns from some that not enough time has passed since Des died. In my heart I felt that I could wait twenty years, but nothing was ever going to bring Des back to life. The best way I can honor her, is to go on living and share my life with the woman God has brought for this last part of the journey.

Becky and I share a new love with new challenges and new joys. Our life is a patchwork quilt that is being designed by our Heavenly Father, and is a gift to share without reservation.

CHAPTER TEN
ANSWERING THE CALL TO TELL THE TRUTH

Life's journey consists of days, weeks and months that flow together toward an unknown destination. We attempt to direct the path, bordered by our limited understanding of God, truth and justice. The further along the path I journey, the more convinced I am that speaking out for being Gay and Christian has nothing to do with being right, it has to do with being faithful to the God who has chosen to dwell within my heart and guide my life.

A year has come and gone since the day Becky and I stood on that Beach in Kauai and committed ourselves to one another and to living out God's truth as Christian and lesbian. We have found that living the truth sometimes makes others uncomfortable, but it is always the truth that sets us free to experience God's love in a redeeming way.

During the past year, I have committed myself to speaking the truth to Christian friends who do not embrace homosexual orientation as a gift from God. Many of them feel it is an abomination and something to bring shame rather than freedom. I have chosen to remain in dialogue with those who do not agree with my understanding of the Scripture and the heart of God. My purpose is not to prove that I am right, or that they are wrong, but rather to be part of the bridge of reconciliation.

Luane Beck and Kim Clark have produced the documentary of <u>God and Gays: Bridging the Gap.</u> (<u>www.godandgaysthemovie.com</u>) It is being shown at film festivals and churches around the country. The truth is being spoken by this film.

I have spoken in churches, at a conference for the film and done newspaper and radio interviews. My story of the exodus from Exodus carries with it a message of hope for a community of people who have been told they didn't have a chance in hell of making it to heaven.

The Exodus International newsletter still proclaims on it's masthead that "…the biblical truth that freedom from homosexuality is possible when Jesus is Lord of one's life." I am grieved that the implication is Jesus cannot be Lord in the life of a person with a homosexual orientation. **This is a broken truth.**

In the July 2006 newsletter, Alan Chambers wrote that "We believe that it is essential for those personally struggling with homosexuality to get connected in the local Body of Christ. Nothing is more important for long term success and healing than being a part of a transparent and committed community where they can know and be known. Counseling, support groups and books are amazing tools, but homosexuality is a relational problem that is healed through healthy relationships." Alan assumes that homosexuality is something to be healed, and that someone who is homosexual is not part of a community of faith and does not experience healthy relationships. **This is a broken Truth**

Each newsletter speaks of the sinfulness of homosexuality, the homosexual agenda, and recounts the scandals of the 30 year history of Exodus. It speaks of a statistic of upwards of 70% of those who come for help either go back to homosexuality or remain bound by their struggle. He attributes this bondage of a lack of a loving truthful community in the local church.

I suspect that the percentage is well upwards of 70%. The issue that homosexual orientation is a God given gift, and was never intended to be something to be healed, changed or delivered from, is not addressed. **Alan's verbiage presents a Broken Truth**

Words are strange. If they are spoken by someone in a position of authority, they are received as truth. The particular Bible teaching that each of us embraces will either support or reject the whole truth from God's word that Jesus never once addressed the topic of homosexuality. Never once did He say that people with a homosexual orientation were to be encouraged to change their behavior, that they were an abomination or that they were flawed and not fit for the kingdom of God! Not once did that message come from the lips of my Lord and Savior Jesus Christ. So, why do we have anyone in Exodus or any pulpit across the world trying to impose change, condemnation or shame upon those gifted with a homosexual orientation? The whole, complete and unfragmented truth is simple to understand.

John 3:17 KJV. <u>For God sent not his son into the world to condemn the world</u>

<u>But that the world through Him, might be saved.</u>

Jesus himself declared in John 8:31 and 32 NIV that:…<u>If you hold to my teaching, you are really my disciples. Then you will know the **truth,** and the **truth will** set you free.</u>

Throughout the New Testament Scriptures, Jesus talks about love and truth, and grace. He died on the cross to bring us into relationship with the Father. His blood that was shed over 2000 years ago paid the price for every person, every sin, every time. This is my belief and my completed truth.

In the Bible, the Exodus refers to coming out of a desert experience and leaving behind the years of bondage to Pharaoh. It was coming into the Promised Land.

Exodus International has taken the name and the image to show how you can come out of homosexual bondage and orientation and enter the promised land of heterosexuality. They admit it is a long journey and there are causalities along the way. Support groups have been established in almost every denomination and state as well as many foreign countries.

People of all ages, broken by the guilt and shame for failure to overcome their homosexual orientation, seek out the support groups and commit to follow rigid guidelines of restraint in order to change their behavior. They are supported by Bible reading and prayer, and others who are on the same journey. The arrival at the Promised Land is an illusion for most of the men and women on the journey, because the premise is faulty. **God will not change an orientation that he has given to His gay and lesbian children.**

I directed Paraklete, an ex-gay referral ministry for several years. I was on the fast tract to national leadership, and was a poster child of proof that the program works. I was free of homosexual feelings and attractions, because I was so busy in ministry that I was emotionally numb, not healed.

I was a licensed minister in the Foursquare Church and spoke at conferences across the nation on behalf of Exodus. It wasn't until Des and I met that I began to search the Scriptures and challenge the teaching and concepts that has been passed on to me by other Exodus leaders. I became convinced that God could not go against His own nature. God is true to Himself, and just to His children. He could not create someone with a homosexual orientation and then condemn that person for acting on those instincts. He could not call something sinful that is His own creation. God not only speaks truth, God is truth, just as He is love.

I recently discovered a book that changed my life and put the Exodus experience in perspective. It is a children's book, titled, "Old Turtle and the Broken Truth" by Douglas Wood. It was published in 2003.

Briefly, it tells the story of something falling from heaven and breaking apart as it landed. A piece was found by certain people. They thought it was beautiful and amazing, and soon began to worship it. It had a message of truth written on it, and the more they worshiped that truth, it became the only truth. It read, "You are loved." The story goes on to tell how battles were waged to protect their truth, and no one was allowed to question its validity. A young girl set off on a journey to find Old Turtle, who in her aged wisdom knew everything. The little girl found the turtle and eventually the other half of the broken truth. She brought it back to the people and when they put it together with their half, it read, "You are loved, and so are they"!

This concept illustrated for me the teachings of Exodus. God does desire wholeness and healing for all of us, but that is not for our sexuality. There are areas of brokenness in my life that God has healed, and the more whole I became; the more I was able to embrace my homosexual orientation. As the truth of His acceptance and love filled my heart, I was able to share in healthy relationships and function in my faith community.

As a child, I was told that sticks and stones may break my bones, but that names would never hurt me. That was one of the first broken truths that I believed. I spent my life being wounded by rejection and cutting names that were intended to separate me from the saving grace of Jesus Christ. Words like sinful, perverted and an abomination to God have been used against the Gay community to separate us from the heart of God. Exodus has used those words for over 30 years, and perpetrated a broken truth myth.

Love, God's love, makes room for inclusiveness. Love enlarges the borders of our hearts and lives. Love keeps no score of wrongs according to I Corinthians chapter 13.

I have learned that embracing a broken truth will keep my spirit broken and wounded. When I was able to see the nature of God, and know Him, I also realized that I didn't have to fight against the teachers of brokenness. I was free to live and love as the woman God created me to be, embracing my sexual orientation as His gift to me.

Speaking the whole truth means that I can encourage everyone to know God and His love, and not have to fight against the hurtful words that are spewed from so many pulpits across this land. It means speaking out for love and justice and letting God take care of His kids that claim to speak for Him on this sensitive topic. The Gospel is the good news and speaks to the whole truth, of His love.

I am committed to living my life in such a way that people will see God's love in my heart and know that I am His beloved daughter.

I wrote to Alan Chambers at the Exodus office recently. I asked him why we have to be so divisive when it comes to this one topic that Jesus never addressed. There are so many topics that we can agree upon, that it seems we have no right to bring condemnation where Jesus has not brought condemnation. He agreed that we should have a message of reconciliation and not of hatred or condemnation. We have agreed to disagree on our understanding of sexuality, however I think it will become clear when we are all standing before the throne of grace.

My call, which is shared and supported by my life partner, Becky, is to speak grace and walk in love toward all God's children.

Our journey continues, as does my process of grieving the death of my former partner. Des taught me many things but the most important thing is that "At the name of Jesus, every knee will bow, and every tongue will confess that Jesus Christ is Lord, to the Glory of God, the Father. (Philippians 2: 10 & 11)

Onward!

Notes

---

1. According to Elaine Sundby who hosts this site:

The primary purpose of the web site is to be *"An affirming gay Christian (GLBT) site dedicated to…"Building (ALL) the Body of Christ in Love!"* The website contains three key things:

The largest and most up-to-date Welcoming Christian directory in the world (we update it daily and personally email every church in the directory to confirm their welcoming status).

One of the largest gay affirming Christian bulletin boards in the world—there is only one I know of other that's larger. Our current membership stands at close to 2,000 members. This will go down soon though as we cull out members who no longer visit the site.

To provide a rich resource of materials to help someone who is struggling with reconciling their sexual orientation with their Christian faith ("Gay and Christian?"). What we don't have within our website we link to. As far as I've seen there is nothing larger and more complete on the web today as far as a resource for articles, studies etc…concerning this subject.

The web site contains numerous other items however these sections are considered slightly secondary to the 3 primary services we provide. Some of the other features of the website are:

A web magazine ("The Word") that contains loads of excellent articles on a wide range of topics and study materials

"La Puerta" where the articles and the "Gay and Christian?" series is translated into Spanish.

"Events" which shows the national and international gay and Christian conferences that are happening.

"**Praise and Worship**" which contains a rich gallery of Christian art created by and large by the people from the bulletin board.

"**Bookstore**" which contains her book, <u>Calling the Rainbow</u> <u>Nation</u> <u>home</u>, and books from well over 150 other authors. It's quite an amazing library all of which was derived from suggestions from the bulletin board when we posed the question: "What book(s) have changed your life?" It *is* an amazing collection of resources for the Christian/Gay community. www.gaychurch.org

2. Kim Clark and Luane Beck have a web site for their documentary film, God and Gays, Bridging the Gap. (www.godandgaysthemovie.com)

3. Mel White, Author of Stranger at the Gate, to be gay and Christian in America and Religion Gone Bad: the Hidden Dangers of the Christian Right is also co founder and president of Soulforce, Inc. an organization committed to ending religious-based bigotry against gay and lesbian Americans. (www.soulforce.org)

4. Ralph Blair is the head of Evangelicals Concerned. (www.ecwr.org) They are one group that is committed to building safe places for the GLBT community

5. Dr.Tricia J. McMahon, Founder of HERS Breast Cancer Foundation…can be contacted at tricia@HERSfund.org.

6. Whosoever: An Online Magazine for GLBT Christians. Candace Chellew-Hodge Founder/Editor

http://www.whoseover.org

ABOUT THE AUTHOR

This book should have been written fifteen years ago. It is a sequel to my "testimony" <u>Long Road to Love</u> that was published by Chosen books in 1985. I was a leader of an Exodus International Ministry, and speaker at conferences around the country. I was the "ex-lesbian" poster child and believed that the absence of feelings made me a heterosexual woman. I loved my Lord Jesus Christ (and still do) and was determined to support other Christians who struggled with homosexuality and help them find complete healing. I spent almost 15 years on this quest. I was the assistant pastor of a Foursquare Church, director of counseling, author of three books, speaker on such shows as Jerry Springer, Sally Jessie Raphael, CBS 48 hours and other national shows declaring my healing and deliverance from homosexuality.

In my quest for acceptance, I became the authority that others sought. I had all the answers.

I acknowledge now that the unconditional Love and acceptance of my Heavenly Father has brought me to an understanding of my sexuality and His plan for my life.

All of the people who have loved me, and whom I have loved along the way have brought me to this place of understanding and embracing my homosexual orientation. I am who I am, and the God who created me, loves and accepts me, just as I am.

696800

Made in the USA